P9-ECS-896

Happy Home

TWENTY-ONE SEWING AND CRAFT PROJECTS
TO PRETTY UP YOUR HOME

BY JENNIFER PAGANELLI

Creator of Sis Boom Fabrics

with DOLIN O'SHEA

Photographs by TIM GEANEY

CHRONICLE BOOKS

SAN FRANCISCO

Copyright © 2012 by Jennifer Paganelli.
Photographs copyright © 2012 by Tim Geaney.

All rights reserved. No part of this book may be reproduced
in any form without written permission from the publisher.

Library of Congress Cataloging-in-Publication Data:
Paganelli, Jennifer.
Happy home : twenty-one sewing and craft projects to pretty up your home /
Jennifer Paganelli ; with Dolin O'Shea ; photographs by Tim Geaney.
p. cm.
ISBN 978-0-8118-7445-8
1. House furnishings. 2. Machine sewing. I. O'Shea, Dolin. II. Title.
TT387.P34 2012
646.2'044—dc23

Manufactured in China
DESIGN BY DESIGN ARMY

1 3 5 7 9 10 8 6 4 2

CHRONICLE BOOKS LLC
680 Second Street
San Francisco, California 94107
www.chroniclebooks.com

To my amazing husband, PETER; my two awesome children,
MATTHEW and KATIE; my beloved assistant, MADELINE RHODES; and
our dog, GEORGE, for their endless contributions, love, support,
and reminders every day that happiness is right here in
front of me. To my BROTHER and SISTERS and the MOTHER who
taught us that a happy home resides in the heart.

"The more you strive and search for happiness
the more you overlook the possibility that
it is here already."

—ROBERT HOLDEN

Contents

Introduction

AT THE CORE OF ANY HAPPY HOME IS LOVE. This book is all about expressing love with handmade projects and creating a happy home—a home that feels like a warm hug and brings a smile to your face.

No matter what sort of space you have, you'll find projects in these pages that will add cheer to your home. This book is not about creating a magazine-worthy, perfectly appointed, perfectly decorated home. Your home may not be perfect. Mine certainly isn't. The secret to crafting a happy home is to let go of perfectionism and let your creativity flow. Work with what you have instead of getting bogged down by what you don't have. Take risks. You may be surprised with the results.

In these pages, I've included a wide range of projects—from a sweet garden hat to a cozy dog bed, to beautiful bedding. Each project offers easy-to-follow directions. You'll find helpful information to get you started and tips on kitting out your sewing basket. You'll also find diagrams and photographs throughout to help you achieve picture-perfect results. The pattern pocket up front holds the pattern pieces themselves.

Play around with fabrics and don't be afraid to mix and match colors. Radiant hues lend such vibrancy to decor. Have fun with these projects!

To me, a happy home is a place where you can truly relax, celebrate, and appreciate the moment. If I held out for absolute perfection in my home, I'd drive myself crazy, and worst of all I'd be too preoccupied to savor the most meaningful moments: quiet time with the kids, getting messy with the dog, neighborhood walks with my husband, and conversations with my girlfriends. Try to remember that you are right where you are supposed to be, and that is where happiness lies. We are all unique and that should show in what we create. Have fun.

Here's to enjoying your Happy Home!

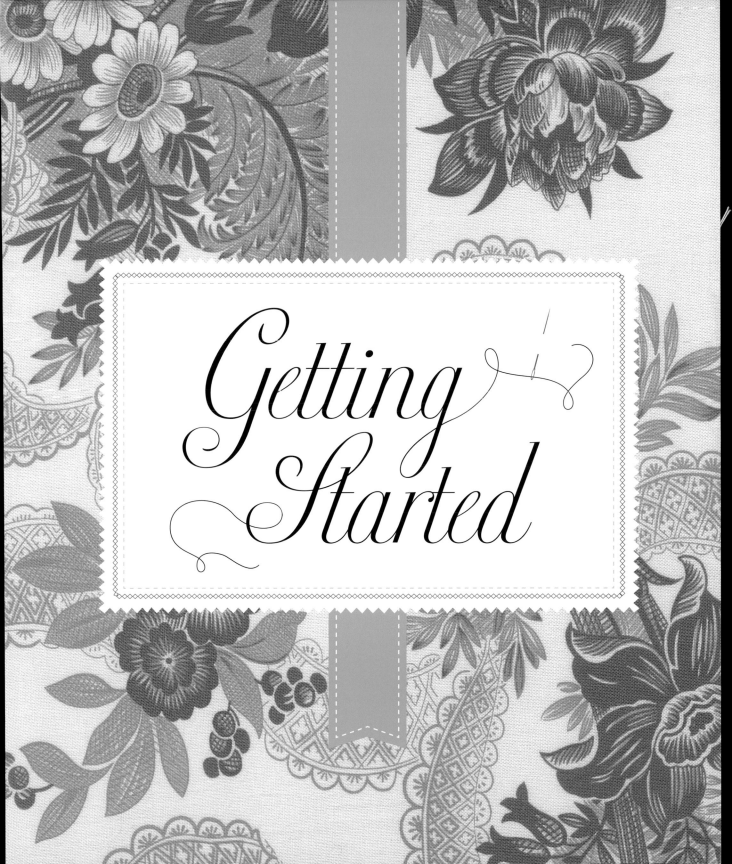

Getting Started

SEWING BASKET BASICS

Here are the items you will need to keep in your sewing basket or your creative space:

- Assortment of hand sewing and machine sewing needles
- Clear grid ruler
- Iron and ironing board
- Safety pins
- Scissors for fabric
- Seam ripper
- Sewing machine
- Small-gauge string or crochet cotton
- Straight pins
- Tape measure
- Turning tool (The tip of a knitting needle or a chopstick will work, too.)
- Water-soluble fabric marker and/or chalk pencil

The items below are not necessary, but they are nice to have around:

- Rotary cutter, cutting mat, and ruler (These items are a must if you will be doing a lot of patchwork projects, like the Madeline Quilt, Jimbo Jumbo Dog Bed, and Playful Pattern Pillow.)
- Tracing paper (This is very handy if you want to use the patterns provided in multiple sizes. Just trace the size/s you want on the tracing paper and cut out to use as the sewing pattern.)

CRAFT CABINET BASICS

- Dual-temperature glue gun and extra glue sticks
- Fine-tip permanent marker (such as a Sharpie)
- Masking tape
- Scissors for paper
- White all-purpose glue (such as Elmer's)
- Tool box outfitted with basic equipment (including hammer, screwdrivers, power drill with bits, and metal tape measure)

TIPS FOR FABRIC SELECTION

The fabric yardage given for these projects allows for a small amount of shrinkage. Extra yardage is not provided for matching prints at seams. If you have a bold pattern or large print that you would like to match, a basic rule of thumb is to buy extra yardage that equals the pattern repeat, for every fabric panel you will need. For example, if you are making Dorothy's Drapery and your pattern repeat is 18 in/46 cm, you need four fabric panels to make the two drapes. Multiply 18 in/46 cm by 4 = 72 in/184 cm. You will need to buy 2 extra yd/m for your project.

GENERAL NOTES FOR ALL PROJECTS

- Preshrink all fabrics before using. To preshrink fabric, wash, dry, and press according to the manufacturer's instructions. If a fabric is dry-clean only, have it dry-cleaned before using.

- Feel free to be creative when choosing fabrics—mix and match to your heart's content. You can use different prints and patterns together in one project. In each project, the yardage requirements are broken down for each component. For instance, a project might require three different fabrics, and the yardage requirements are listed separately for each fabric. If you want to use only one fabric, add up the three yardage requirements to get the total yardage needed. A word of caution: If you want to mix and match different types of fabric, make sure that all can be cleaned the same way.

- All pattern pieces and cut measurement dimensions include seam allowances, unless otherwise mentioned in the instructions. Seam allowances are given in the instructions for each project.

- All cut measurement dimensions are given as length by width, for example: Cut two 20-by-14 in/ 50-by-35.5 cm rectangles. The length measurement (20 in/50 cm) is along the length grain of the fabric, and the width measurement (14 in/35.5 cm) is along the cross grain of the fabric.

- Before starting a project, have all the necessary materials, sewing basket items, and craft cabinet items ready and available for use.

- When cutting out all pieces, make sure to transfer all notches to the fabric by making a small cut for each into the seam allowance only.

- At the start and end of each seam, backstitch *(see page 19)* a few stitches to secure the seam and to make sure it doesn't come undone. The only time you don't want to backstitch is when you're basting.

- Most of the sewing in this book is done with a sewing machine, unless otherwise stated. A few projects require small amounts of hand sewing to finish them off.

- For all the sewing projects that require pressing, please be sure to follow the iron's and/or the fabric manufacturer's recommendations for temperature.

- When cutting out the various projects, use the appropriate type of scissors. Cut fabric with only your fabric scissors and cut paper with only your paper scissors. Paper dulls the scissor blades very quickly, so it is best to have different scissors for each of your cutting needs.

- Please use caution when working with a dual-temperature glue gun and follow the manufacturer's instructions.

- For any project that uses glue, let the glue dry completely before moving on to the next step or using the item.

GLOSSARY

BABY HEM

A baby hem is a very small hem that is folded over twice. It is used often on lightweight fabrics and on any hem where you don't want a lot of bulk. To make a baby hem on a raw edge, place one row of stitching ¼ in/6 mm from the raw edge. Fold the fabric over, **wrong** sides together, along the stitch line and press. Place a second row of stitching very close (no more than ⅛ in/3 mm) to the first fold/first stitch line. Trim off the excess fabric close to the second row of stitching. Fold the fabric over, one more time, along this second stitch line and press. Edge stitch along the inner folded edge.

BACKSTITCH

Backstitching is done at the start and end of each seam. When beginning a seam, sew a few stitches forward, and then reverse your sewing machine and go back over the first stitches. Continue sewing forward until the end of the seam, and then sew a few stitches in reverse to go over the final few stitches. The backstitch is also a hand-sewing stitch. For more information, please see Hand-Tied Quilting, on page 24.

BASTE

Done by machine or by hand, basting is a temporary stitch that is usually removed when an item is completed. It comes in handy when you need to keep layers of fabric in place before stitching them together permanently. To baste by machine, set the straight stitch length to the longest setting and sew as usual. Most of the basting done in this book is by machine. The only project that you may want to baste by hand is the Madeline Quilt. To baste by hand, do a simple running stitch, but with longer stitches than usual. For more information, please see Running Stitch, on page 25.

BIAS

The bias grain runs diagonally, at a 45-degree angle, between the length and cross grain of the fabric. To cut on the bias, make sure the grain line on the pattern is placed at a 45-degree angle to the selvage. When fabric is cut on the bias, it becomes slightly stretchy and has a bit of give.

BINDING

Binding is made with strips of fabric that encase the raw edges of a project to create a finished edge. For the projects in this book, the binding strips will be cut either on the cross grain or on the bias. The strips cut on the cross grain are used on straight edges. The strips cut on the bias are used on curved edges. Binding strips may be folded in different ways to achieve different effects. Three types are used in this book:

1 Single-fold binding. This binding has a fold along each long edge. It is used

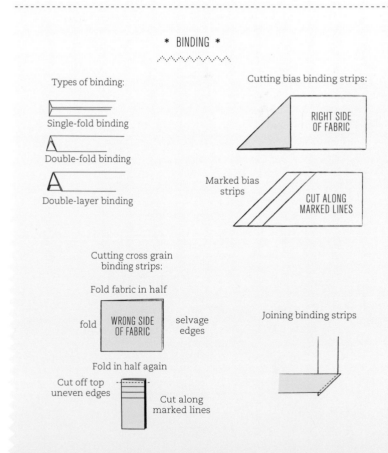

* BINDING *

Types of binding:

Single-fold binding

Double-fold binding

Double-layer binding

Cutting bias binding strips:

RIGHT SIDE OF FABRIC

Marked bias strips

CUT ALONG MARKED LINES

Cutting cross grain binding strips:

Fold fabric in half

fold WRONG SIDE OF FABRIC selvage edges

Fold in half again

Cut off top uneven edges

Cut along marked lines

Joining binding strips

to finish edges and to add casings. This type will only be seen on the **wrong** side of a project in this book. *(See illustration on page 19.)*

2   Double-fold binding. This type has the same two folds as for the single-fold binding, but the binding strip is then folded lengthwise, down the center, and both edges are aligned. This binding is used to encase raw edges and is seen on both sides of the project. *(See illustration on page 19.)*

3   Double-layer binding. This binding is folded in half lengthwise, aligning the long raw edges with **wrong** sides together. The raw edges are sewn along the edge of the **right** side of the project, and the entire binding is folded to the **wrong** side, so that it encases the raw edges, and then is stitched down on the **wrong** side. This binding is more durable and is used mainly to bind the edges of quilts. *(See illustration on page 19.)*

The instructions for each project will specify on which grain to cut the binding strips and how they should be folded.

INSTRUCTIONS FOR CUTTING BINDING STRIPS

On the bias: Lay the fabric **right**-side up on a flat surface. Pick up one corner and fold the fabric over, placing **right** sides together and aligning the selvage edge with the cut edge of the fabric. Carefully cut along the diagonal fold. Beginning at the cut edge, measure the width specified in the project and draw a line with marker or chalk. Continue measuring from each line until you have enough strips for the length of binding called for in the instructions. Cut the strips along the drawn lines. *(See illustration on page 19.)*

On the cross grain: Lay the fabric **right**-side up on a flat surface. Fold the fabric in half, with **right** sides together, aligning the selvage edges. Fold in half again, aligning the fold with the selvage. Square off the top raw edge by cutting straight across at a 90-degree angle from the selvage. Beginning at the squared-off edge, measure the width specified in the project and draw a line. Continue measuring from each line until you have enough strips for the length of binding called for in the instructions. Cut the strips along the drawn lines, and then cut each end at a 45-degree angle, making sure to remove the selvage edges. *(See illustration on page 19.)*

INSTRUCTIONS FOR JOINING BINDING STRIPS

Lay strips perpendicular to each other, with **right** sides together, aligning short ends. Sew the ends together using a ¼-in/6-mm seam allowance. Press the seam open and trim off the small points of fabric that extend past the seam. After all the binding strips are joined, you will need to fold and press the joined strip into one of the three types of binding mentioned above. Each project that uses binding will specify which type to use.

BLANKET STITCH

This versatile stitch finishes an edge so it doesn't fray. It can be used as a decorative detail, or it can act as a base for adding crochet or knitted trims

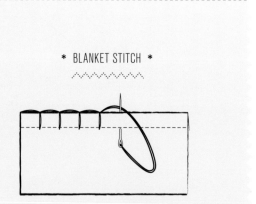

* BLANKET STITCH *

onto a fabric, which is how we use it in this book. The stitch looks a bit like upside-down, backward, interlocking Ls. Some sewing machines have a built-in small blanket stitch, but the stitch can also be sewn by hand. To sew by hand, working from left to right, bring your needle and thread up through the fabric anywhere along the top folded edge that you will be stitching. Then pull the needle and thread back down through the fabric (front to back) to the right and below (see Crocheted Pillowcase for exact distance), where the stitching is started, making sure to catch the thread behind the needle. Continue in this manner until finished. *(See illustration on facing page.)*

CLIP SEAM ALLOWANCE

Clipping the seam allowance on curved seams makes it possible for the seam allowance to lay flat on the **wrong** side and creates a smoothly shaped seam on the **right** side. After sewing a curved seam, use very sharp scissors to make small cuts in the seam allowance. Be very careful not to cut the stitching. On a sharply curved seam, you will need to make more clips than on a slightly curved seam.

CUT ON THE FOLD

Some pattern pieces and cut measurement dimensions represent only half of the complete piece. You are meant to fold your fabric before cutting so you will have a full-sized piece after cutting. If a pattern piece says to cut on the fold, fold the fabric and place the edge of the pattern marked "Place on Fold" along the folded edge. Cut around the outer edges. When you finish cutting and unfold the fabric, each half will be a mirror image of the other half. If a cut measurement dimension says to cut on the fold, the width measurement will represent only half of the total width needed. When cut out and unfolded, the total width measurement will be correct. In very rare cases, instructions may tell you to cut the length measurement on the fold. Please refer to the fabric layout diagrams given for each project.

EDGE STITCH

Edge stitching is a form of top-stitching that is done very close to an edge or a seam—usually $1/16$ in/ 2 mm to $1/8$ in/3 mm from the edge or seam. For more information, see Topstitch, on page 26.

FINISHING EDGES

You'll want to finish the edges on any seam allowance that's exposed on the inside of a garment or on an item that will be washed frequently. This is necessary for a clean, finished look and to keep the edges of the fabric from fraying. There are many ways to finish the edges of a seam allowance, but the three

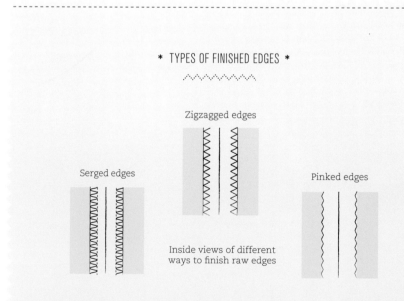

* TYPES OF FINISHED EDGES *

Zigzagged edges

Serged edges

Pinked edges

Inside views of different ways to finish raw edges

most common methods are serging with a serger, using a zigzag stitch with a sewing machine, or trimming with pinking shears. *(See illustration on page 21.)*

FINGER PRESS

To finger press, just run your finger along the seam to press the seam allowance in a particular direction, as the instructions indicate in a project. This is a quick way to set a seam, without having to press it with an iron. Once the seams have been sewn, you will want to use an iron to permanently set your seams.

FREE-MOTION QUILTING

This is one of the many ways to sew the three layers of a quilt together. To do free-motion quilting, you will need to make sure that your sewing machine can drop the feed dogs and has a darning foot. With the feed dogs dropped, you're able to move the fabric in any direction, not just forward and backward as in regular sewing. Because you can move the fabric in any direction, you can "draw" or stitch any type of design you wish. Free-motion quilting is a lot of fun, but can take some practice. Try it on some fabric scraps first, to get a feel for it. If you need more information, look online for some great tutorials and resources.

FRENCH SEAM

French seams are seams that have the raw edges fully enclosed within the seam allowance. They are very simple to do and provide a totally finished edge on your seam allowances. This type of seam is

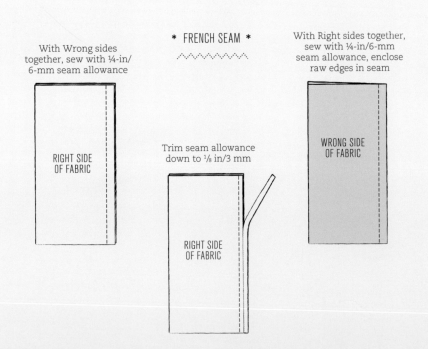

With Wrong sides together, sew with ¼-in/ 6-mm seam allowance

* FRENCH SEAM *

With Right sides together, sew with ¼-in/6-mm seam allowance, enclose raw edges in seam

RIGHT SIDE OF FABRIC

Trim seam allowance down to ⅛ in/3 mm

RIGHT SIDE OF FABRIC

WRONG SIDE OF FABRIC

perfect for finishing raw edges on sheer fabric or for any seam that could be visible on the outside of an item. However, French seams don't work well on curved seams. For the projects in this book, you can follow these directions: With the **wrong** sides together, sew a ¼-in/6-mm seam allowance. Then trim seam allowance to ⅛ in/3 mm. Press the seam open, then press to one side. Fold the pieces so the **right** sides are together and press so the seam is on the fold of the fabric. Sew together with a ¼-in/6-mm seam allowance. This will enclose the raw edge within the seam allowance. *(See illustration on facing page.)*

GATHERING

Gathering is done when you want to attach a larger piece of fabric to a smaller piece—for instance, when you sew a ruffle to the edge of a pillow. There are a few ways to gather fabric, and we have two methods in this book. In all the project instructions, we recommend gathering method two, because most of the gathering is on larger areas. Feel free to use method one or another preferred method.

METHOD ONE

This method works best when gathering smaller areas, mainly on clothing. Run one row of basting stitches ⅛ in/3 mm above and another row of basting stitches ⅛ in/3 mm below the called-for seam allowance in the section that is to be gathered. For example, if the seam allowance is ⅝ in/16 mm, you would stitch a basting seam at ½ in/12 mm from the raw edge and another ¾ in/2 cm from the raw edge. After stitching the 2 rows of basting stitches, pick up only the bobbin threads and gently pull; the fabric will gather up along your stitches. To help remember which threads are the bobbin threads, use a different color thread for the bobbin. Once the piece has the required amount of gathering, pin it to the piece to which it will be sewn, according to the pattern and/or instructions. Distribute the gathers evenly, and then sew the 2 pieces together. After sewing the pieces together, you will need to remove the visible basting threads with a seam ripper. *(See illustration.)*

METHOD TWO

This method is best used when you need to gather a large area, like a ruffle to the edge of a pillow. The method has more durable results; there is no chance of breaking the bobbin threads as there is with method one when used on large areas. You'll need some nonstretchy, small-gauge string (crochet cotton works really well) and zigzag stitch capabilities on your sewing machine. Set the zigzag stitch width to the widest setting and the zigzag length to the longest setting (as for basting). Lay the string on the fabric and center it beneath the presser foot. You'll want the zigzag stitching to be placed ¼ in/6 mm closer to the raw edge than the called-for seam

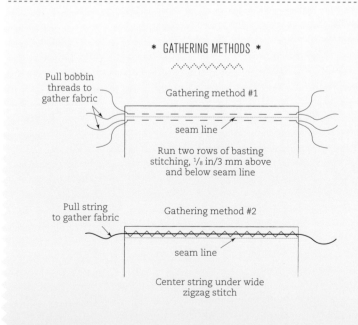

* GATHERING METHODS *

Pull bobbin
threads to
gather fabric

Gathering method #1

seam line

Run two rows of basting
stitching, ⅛ in/3 mm above
and below seam line

Pull string
to gather fabric

Gathering method #2

seam line

Center string under wide
zigzag stitch

allowance. For example, if the seam allowance is ⅝ in/16 mm, work the zigzag stitch ⅜ in/1 cm from the raw edge, being careful to keep the string centered under the stitching; you don't want it to get caught by the needle. After working the zigzag stitch over the string, pin the soon-to-be-gathered piece to the piece to which it will be sewn according to the instructions, aligning at necessary points or seams. Then, pick up the string ends and gently start pulling. Pull until gathered to the correct size, distributing gathers evenly, and pin in place. Sew the pieces together, making sure not to catch the string in the stitching. Once the pieces are sewn together, you should be able to pull the string out. Since the zigzag stitches are on the seam allowance, and not seen from the **right** side, it's up to you whether or not to remove them with a seam ripper. *(See illustration on page 23.)*

GRAIN OF FABRIC

The grain of the fabric is the direction of the woven threads that make up fabric. Length grain runs the length of the fabric, from cut edge to cut edge. Cross grain runs the width of the fabric, from selvage edge to selvage edge. The bias grain runs diagonally across the length and cross grain *(see Bias, on page 19)*. All pattern pieces in this book are marked with a grain line. This line is there to help you align each pattern piece correctly on the fabric grain. All the pattern grain lines should be aligned along the length grain, unless otherwise noted in the instructions.

HAND-TIED QUILTING

Hand tying is a great way to quickly finish a quilt. You will need a hand sewing needle and some embroidery floss. With the **right** side of the quilt facing up and the quilt sandwich assembled, take a small backstitch at each intersection between squares. Cut the floss, leaving about a 2-in/5-cm tail of floss at each side of the backstitch. Tie the tails in a knot and trim the tails so they are even. *(See illustration.)*

NOTCHES

These are the small triangular markings on the cutting lines on the pattern pieces. Notches are used as a guide for matching up seams and for placement of items along the seam.

PIVOT

Pivoting is used to change direction in sewing: to turn a corner or continue the stitching in a different direction. To pivot, you stop stitching, with the needle in the down position; this holds the fabric in place. Then you raise the presser foot and rotate the fabric in the direction you want to sew. Drop the presser foot and continue sewing.

* HAND-TIED QUILTING *

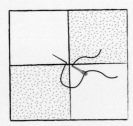

At each interstection take
a small backstitch

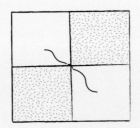

Tie ends into a knot
over the backstitch

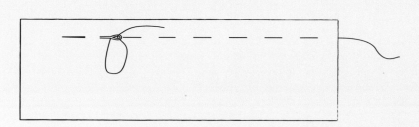

* RUNNING STITCH AS USED WHEN BASTING BY HAND *

RUNNING STITCH

A running stitch is one of the most basic hand stitches you can do. It isn't a particularly strong stitch, so it is best suited to use as basting. To do a running stitch, insert the needle into the fabric and then pull back up through fabric at regular intervals. *(See illustration above.)*

SATIN STITCH

This type of stitching can be done by hand or by machine. We will only do a satin stitch by machine in this book. Satin stitching by machine is a dense form of the zigzag stitch. Set the stitch width to the desired setting and set the stitch length to a very short setting. This is a great way to attach fabric appliqué pieces to a base fabric. *(See illustration on page 26.)*

SEAM ALLOWANCE

The seam allowance is the area of fabric between the sewn seam and the raw edge. The seam allowance can be pressed to one side or the other, or it can be pressed open using an iron.

SLIP STITCH

The slip stitch is a hand-sewing stitch that is nearly invisible. It is perfect for closing up an opening. It's also used for attaching a folded edge to a single layer of fabric, as on a quilt when the binding is sewn to the back of the quilt. To slip stitch, working from right to left, insert the needle into the top fabric and make a tiny stitch. Then insert the needle into the fold on the bottom fabric, and bring the needle back up through the fold about ¼ in/6 mm away from where it was inserted. *(See illustration on page 26.)*

STITCH IN THE DITCH

Stitching in the ditch is done by sewing directly in the groove formed by a seam. This technique is used to sew all the layers of The Broad Brim hat together. It can also be used to sew the layers of the Madeline Quilt or the Jimbo Jumbo Dog Bed.

TRIM CORNERS

Trimming off the corners reduces the amount of excess seam allowance inside a seam. To trim the excess seam allowance, cut off the allowance close to the seam, being careful not to cut into the seam. When the project is turned **right**-side out, the corners will be sharper and easier to push out.

TOPSTITCH

Topstitching is an additional row or rows of stitching worked near a seam, using a sewing machine. This technique adds a decorative touch and some extra strength. Topstitching should be done with the project **right**-side up, so you can be sure that the stitching is straight and parallel to the seam. You will also want to be sure that the seam allowance, on the **wrong** side, is caught in the top stitching. The instructions in each project will specify how far the topstitching should be placed from the seam.

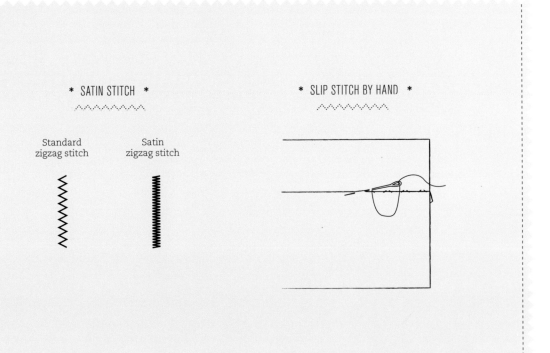

* SATIN STITCH *

Standard zigzag stitch   Satin zigzag stitch

* SLIP STITCH BY HAND *

Decorate

№
1
RACHEL'S RUFFLE PILLOW

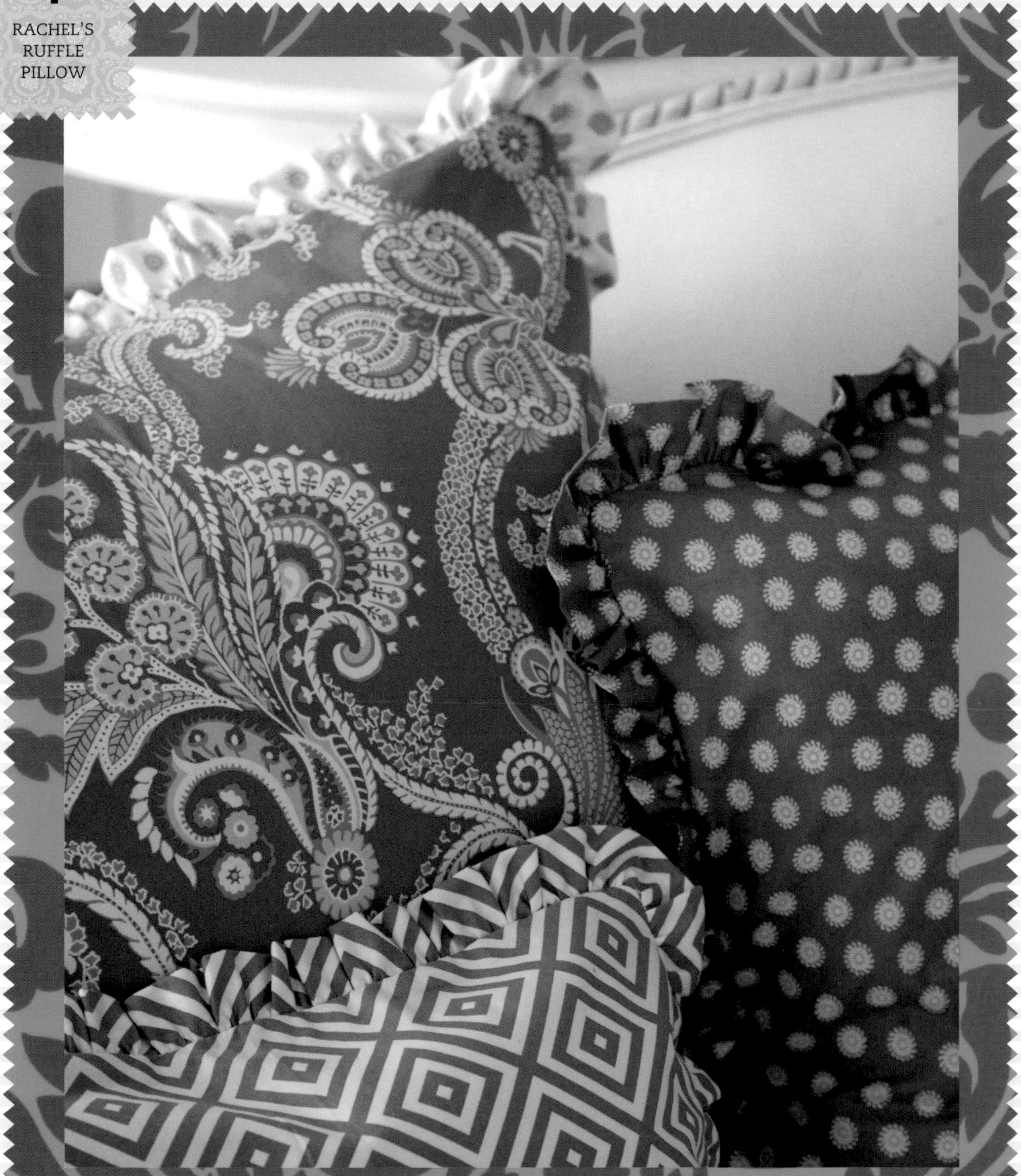

№
2
PLAYFUL PATTERNED PILLOW

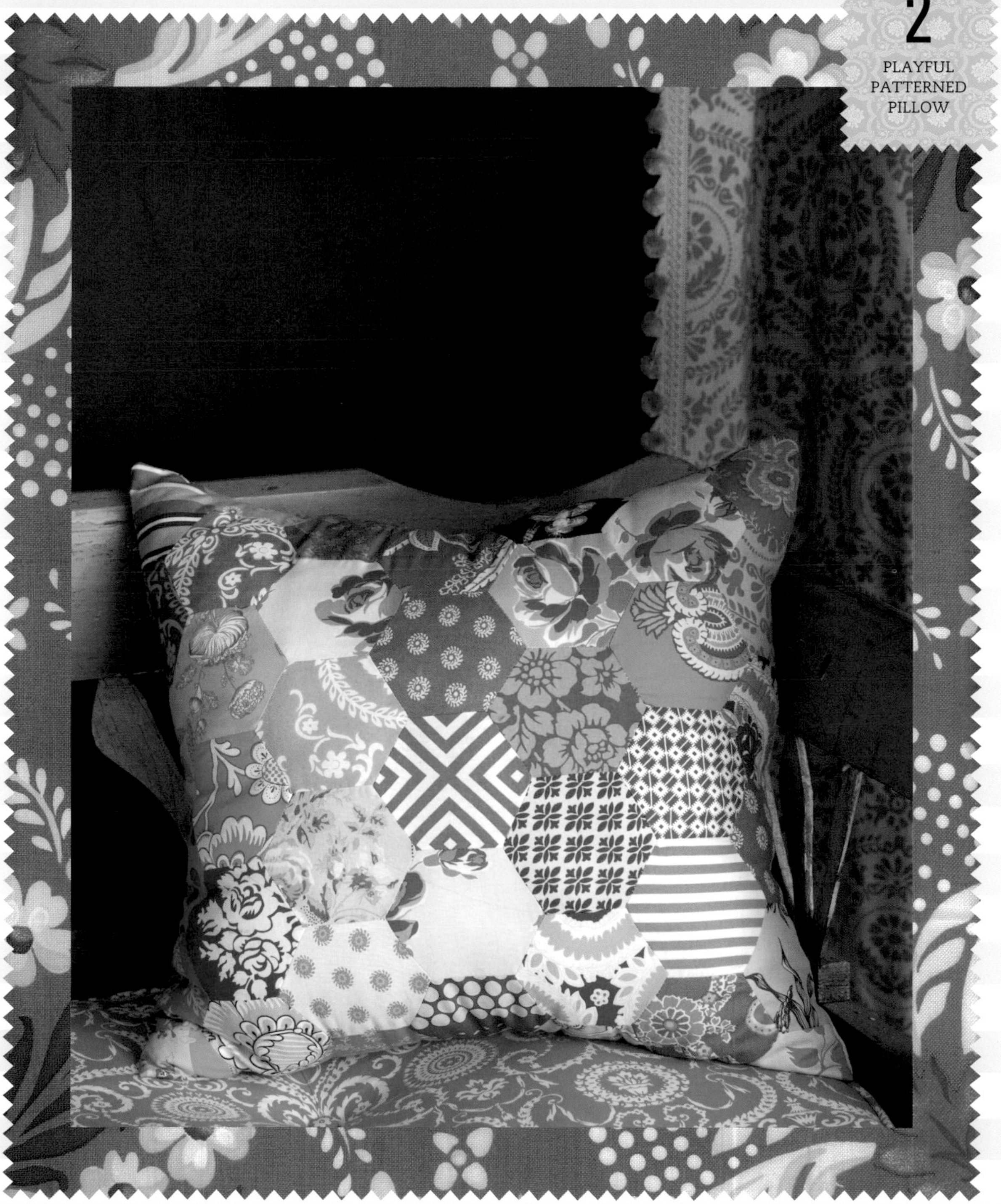

NO
4
DOROTHY'S
DRAPERY

Rachel's Ruffle Pillow

We here at Sis Boom love a good ruffle, but we understand that the guys in our lives may not be as enthusiastic. So here is a simple fold-over ruffle that adds a bit of personality without too much fussiness. This pillow can look great in a formal living room, a cozy bedroom, or a casual family room. You can use playful polka dots, masculine stripes, or modern florals, or mix it up and use two different fabrics.

Finished size (including ruffle):

22-IN/56-CM SQUARE

MATERIALS

- 1¼ yd/1.2 m printed mid-weight cotton fabric (45 in/114 cm wide) for Front and Back
- ⅜ yd/34 cm coordinating mid-weight cotton fabric (45 in/114 cm wide) for Ruffle
- One 20-in/50-cm square pillow insert
- Coordinating thread

FROM THE SEWING BASKET

- Water-soluble fabric marker
- Ruler
- Pins
- Scissors for fabric
- Small-gauge string or crochet cotton

CUTTING

Fold the fabric in half, **right** sides together, and align the selvage edges. Using the fabric marker and the ruler, draw the dimensions below onto the **wrong** side of the fabric.

FROM FRONT AND BACK FABRIC:

Cut one 20-by-10-in/50-by-25-cm rectangle, on the fold.
Cut two 20-by-14-in/50-by-35.5-cm rectangles.

FROM RUFFLE FABRIC:

Cut three 3½-by-21-in/9-by-53-cm rectangles, on the fold.
(See fabric layout diagram.)

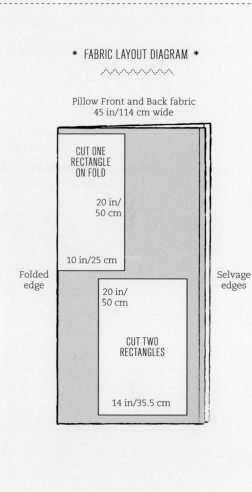

* FABRIC LAYOUT DIAGRAM *

Pillow Front and Back fabric
45 in/114 cm wide

CUT ONE RECTANGLE ON FOLD

20 in/ 50 cm

10 in/25 cm

Folded edge

Selvage edges

20 in/ 50 cm

CUT TWO RECTANGLES

14 in/35.5 cm

Ruffle fabric
45 in/114 cm wide

Folded edge

CUT THREE RECTANGLES ON FOLD

Selvage edges

ASSEMBLE

STEP 1: RUFFLE

A Place 2 Ruffle pieces, **right** sides together, align along 1 of the short ends, and pin. Sew together with a ¼-in/6-mm seam allowance. Align the third Ruffle piece with 1 end of the joined Ruffle pieces, **right** sides together. Sew together with a ¼-in/6-mm seam allowance. You now have 1 long Ruffle piece. Align both short ends of the Ruffle piece, **right** sides together, and pin. Sew together with a ¼-in/6-mm seam allowance. Now the Ruffle piece is a big loop. Press all the seams open. Then fold the Ruffle piece in half lengthwise, **wrong** sides together, align the raw edges, and press.

B Follow the instructions for gathering method two (*see page* 23) along the raw edges of the Ruffle. Don't pull the string to gather. Fold the Ruffle piece flat and clip a ¼-in/6-mm notch at each folded raw edge. Then fold the flattened Ruffle piece in half and clip ¼-in/6-mm notches through all layers of the folded raw edges. You want to have 4 evenly spaced notches along the raw edge, to align with each of the corners of the pillow pieces.

C Pull the string on the Ruffle piece and gather to the approximate size of the outer perimeter of the pillow Front piece.

D Place the Front piece **right**-side up on a flat surface, and pin the Ruffle piece to the Front piece, aligning each of the Ruffle notches to the corners of the Front. Distribute the Ruffle gathers evenly around pillow, pinning as needed. Once you are happy with the Ruffle gathers, baste the Ruffle to all 4 sides of the Front, ⅜ in/1 cm from the raw edges, pivoting at each corner. (*See illustration.*) Clip the gathering string in a few places and pull to remove. Lightly press the Ruffle so the folded edge is lying nicely toward the center of the Front.

STEP 2: BACK AND FINISHING

A With the Back pieces **wrong**-side up on your ironing board, fold 1 long raw edge over ½ in/12 mm and press. Then fold the same edge over another ½ in/12 mm and press again. Repeat on the other Back piece. Pin the hems in place as needed. Edge stitch along the inner folded edges of each Back piece.

B Place the Front piece **right**-side up on a flat surface. Then place 1 Back piece on top of the Front, **right** sides together. Align all the raw edges and make sure that the Back hemmed edge is toward the center of the Front. Pin together. Repeat with the second Back piece on the opposite side of the Front. The Back hemmed edges should overlap about 6 in/15 cm. The Ruffle is now sandwiched between the Front and Back. (*See illustration.*)

C Sew around the perimeter of the pillow cover with a ½-in/12-mm seam allowance. Pivot around each corner as you go. Clip the corners (*see page* 21) and finish the raw edges in your preferred method.

D Turn the pillow cover **right**-side out, through the overlap opening. Press around the outside edges and stuff with the pillow insert.

* STEP 1D *

Baste Ruffle to outside
edges of Front pillow

RIGHT SIDE FRONT PILLOW

Match notches in
Ruffle to corners
of Front pillow

* STEP 2B *

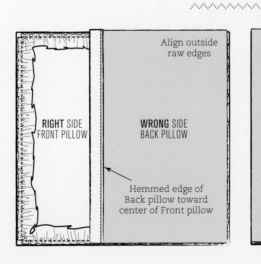

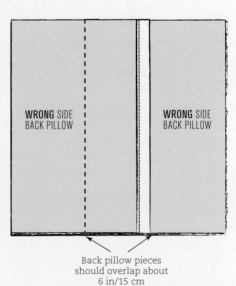

Align outside
raw edges

RIGHT SIDE
FRONT PILLOW

WRONG SIDE
BACK PILLOW

Hemmed edge of
Back pillow toward
center of Front pillow

WRONG SIDE
BACK PILLOW

WRONG SIDE
BACK PILLOW

Back pillow pieces
should overlap about
6 in/15 cm

Playful Patterned Pillow

Take your patchwork up a notch and piece a fabulous pillow cover entirely in hexagons! The best part is that you can whip up this project with your sewing machine. This is an excellent project for practicing precision cutting and sewing.

Finished size:

19 BY 18½ IN/48 BY 47 CM

MATERIALS

- Twelve ⅛-yd/11-cm lengths of different printed mid-weight cotton fabrics (45 in/114 cm wide) for pillow cover
  OR
- Eighty-four 4½-in/11-cm-square random fabric scraps
- One 20-in/50-cm square pillow insert
- Coordinating thread
- 4-in/10-cm square clear template plastic

FROM THE SEWING BASKET

- Water-soluble fabric marker
- Rotary cutter, mat, and ruler
- Pins
- Hand sewing needle

FROM THE CRAFT CABINET

- Masking tape
- Fine-tip permanent marker

TRACING, MARKING, AND CUTTING

Trace the template—Place the template plastic over the hexagon pattern provided in the front pocket of this book. Secure the template plastic with masking tape. With the ruler and the fine-tip permanent marker, trace the hexagon pattern; make sure to trace the grain line, too. Please note that the hexagon pattern does not include the seam allowance. The seam allowance will be added when cutting out the pieces.

Mark the fabric—If using the 12 different fabrics, fold each fabric in half, **right** sides together, and align the selvage edges. Then fold the fabric in half again, and align the fold with the selvage edges. With the water-soluble fabric marker, trace around the template onto the **wrong** side of the fabric 2 times. Make sure to leave at least ½ in/12 mm between the 2 tracings for the seam allowance, and that the grain line of the template is placed along the lengthwise grain of the fabric. Note that after cutting you will end up with 8 hexagon pieces; you will only need 7 of each different print. (*See fabric layout diagram.*)

Use layout for each of the Hexagon fabrics 45 in/ 114 cm wide. Fold fabric so there are four layers

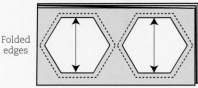

Folded edges

Two Selvage edges and One folded edge

Add ¼-in/6-mm seam allowance, before cutting

Keep hexagons stacked together so that grain lines are aligned

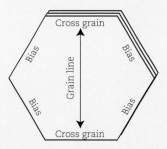

Cross grain

Bias

Bias

Grain line

Bias

Bias

Cross grain

TIP: You can use the extra hexagons to practice sewing them together. This can be confusing at first, but once you see the order of sewing, you'll find it a lot easier. A great tutorial on how to machine piece hexagons is at www.ladyharvatine.com/2010/03/hexagonia.html.

If using fabric scraps, stack 3 or 4 pieces on top of each other, keeping the lengthwise grain aligned. Then trace the hexagon template onto the **wrong** side of the top piece. Make sure to leave at least ¼ in/6 mm of excess fabric on all edges and that the grain line of the template is placed along the lengthwise grain of the fabrics.

Cut the fabric—Place the fabric with the traced hexagons on the cutting mat. Place the ruler over 1 straight edge of a traced hexagon, and align the traced straight edge with a ¼-in/6-mm mark on the ruler. Hold the ruler firmly in place, and with the rotary cutter, cut along the edge of the ruler. Make sure that you cut exactly ¼ in/6 mm from the traced line. Repeat for all sides of each traced hexagon. If using 12 different fabrics, stack the same fabrics together, keeping the grain lines aligned. If using fabric scraps, you can stack them into groupings of similar colors or scale of pattern or from light to dark. The important thing is to keep the grain of the fabric in the same direction. *(See fabric layout diagram on page 43.)*

ASSEMBLE

STEP 1: HEXAGON LAYOUT

A   If you are using 12 different fabrics, we have provided a layout diagram *(see illustration)*, or you can do something totally random. The key is to play around with the layout until you get something that pleases you. You will want to lay the hexagons out in 7 rows with 12 hexagons in each row, keeping the grain lines in the same direction.

B   Once you are happy with your layout, place each row into a stack, keeping the hexagons in the order that you want them sewn together. With masking tape and marker, label the top piece of each stack (1 through 7).

STEP 2: SEW HEXAGONS

TIP: It is very important to keep your seam allowance a consistent ¼ in/6 mm when sewing the hexagons together.

A   Starting with the top 2 hexagons of a stack, place the **right** sides together and sew along 1 of the cross grain edges, using a ¼-in/6-mm seam allowance, and starting and stopping ¼ in/6 mm from each end *(see illustration)*. Please note that keeping ¼ in/6 mm unsewn at the beginning and end of each seam is the key to being able to sew the rows together. If you don't feel comfortable eyeballing these points, use the water-soluble fabric marker to place dots where you need to start and stop the sewing.

B   Take the third hexagon from the stack, place it **right** side together with the second hexagon (the one without the masking tape). Sew together on the cross grain edge with a ¼-in/6-mm seam allowance, starting and stopping ¼ in/6 mm from each end. Repeat this step with each consecutive hexagon in the stack of 12. Press each seam open.

* STEP 1A *

12 different fabrics

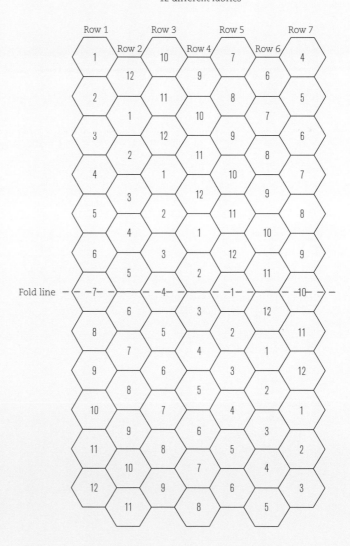

Row 1   Row 2   Row 3   Row 4   Row 5   Row 6   Row 7

Fold line

* STEP 2A *

With hexagons **right** sides together, sew with ¼-in/6-mm seam allowance, starting and stopping ¼-in/6-mm from each edge

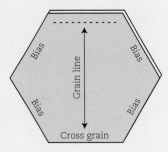

* STEP 2D *

Sew together with ¼-in/6-mm seam allowance, starting and stopping ¼-in/6-mm from each edge

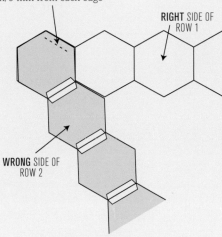

RIGHT SIDE OF ROW 1

WRONG SIDE OF ROW 2

* STEP 2E *

WRONG SIDE OF ROW 2

With seam allowances finger pressed back, sew together with ¼-in/6-mm seam allowance

Row 1 first hexagon folded in half, **right** sides together

RIGHT SIDE OF ROW 1

* STEP 2F *

With seam allowances finger pressed back, sew together with ¼-in/6-mm seam allowance. Start at the edge and stop ¼-in/6-mm from the edge

RIGHT SIDE OF ROW 1

Row 2 first hexagon folded in half, **right** sides together

RIGHT SIDE OF ROW 1

WRONG SIDE OF ROW 2

C   Repeat steps 2A and 2B for each of the 7 rows. Then lay the rows out in numerical order.

D   Take the first 2 rows, and place the top 2 hexagons **right** sides together, aligning the bottom bias edge of the Row 1 hexagon with the top bias edge of the Row 2 hexagon. Sew together with a ¼-in/6-mm seam allowance, starting and stopping ¼ in/6 mm from each end *(see illustration)*. Finger press *(see page 22)* the seam open.

E   Fold the first hexagon from Row 1 in half at the widest point, **right** sides together. This will help align the next bias edges that will be sewn together from Rows 1 and 2. It will be easy to see where to start your sewing at this point, because you will be starting this seam where you ended the last one and finger pressed it open. Sew the bias hexagon edges together with a ¼-in/6-mm seam allowance, stopping where the Row 2 first 2 hexagons are joined. *(See illustration.)* Finger press the seam open.

F   Fold the first hexagon from Row 2 in half at the widest point, **right** sides together. Align the next bias edges that will be sewn together. Start this seam where the previous one ended and sew together with a ¼-in/6-mm seam allowance, stopping ¼ in/6 mm from the end of the top hexagon, which should line up with the intersection of the Row 1 hexagons. *(See illustration.)* Are you starting to see a pattern? Basically, you fold the previously sewn hexagon in half, alternating between the 2 rows each time; this helps align the next edges that should be sewn together. Finger pressing the seams open as you go really helps you see where to start and stop your sewing. Continue in this manner until Rows 1 and 2 are completely sewn together. Repeat for the remaining rows.

G   When all the rows are sewn together, fold the pieced fabric in half lengthwise, **right** sides together. Sew the hexagons together (using the method described in steps 2E and 2F) along the short ends of the pieced fabric, with a ¼-in/6-mm seam allowance. This will create a tube.

H   Press all seams open well with an iron.

STEP 3: FINISHING

A   Fold the tube of pieced hexagons flat, **right** sides together, making sure that the raw edges on the open ends of the tube are aligned. With the ruler and the water-soluble marker, draw a straight line down one of the open ends about ¼ in/6-mm from the innermost raw edges. Pin both layers together along the drawn line. Repeat on other open side.

B   Sew 1 open end closed along the drawn line. On the second open end, sew 2 in/5 cm closed, at the top and bottom of the seam, leaving an opening of about 15 in/38 cm.

C   Cut off the points at each of these seams, leaving an even ⅜-in/1-cm seam allowance. Along the opening, you may want to go back and reinforce all the hexagon joins with a quick backstitch, since the original backstitch can get cut off. Fold and press the edges of the opening back ⅜ in/1 cm, **wrong** sides together.

D   Turn the pillow cover **right**-side out through the opening, then stuff with pillow insert. Using the hand sewing needle and thread, slipstitch the opening closed.

No
3

Express Yourself Appliqué Pillow

What makes a better gift than a sweet phrase appliquéd on a soft pillow? Once you learn the basics of this type of appliqué, there is no end to variations you can create. The letters we used were done freehand, which is another great way to add a personal touch. If you don't feel like drawing your own letters, you can download a free font, such as Headline, at www.dafont.com. The instructions below are for a square pillow, like the one pictured that says "Happy Home." You can make the pillow any shape you like.

Finished size:

20-IN/50-CM SQUARE

MATERIALS

- ⅝ yd/57 cm solid mid-weight cotton canvas or home dec fabric (54 in/137 cm wide) for Front and Back
- 8-by-5-in/20-by-12-cm scraps of printed cotton fabric, a different one for each appliquéd letter
- ¾ yd/70 cm Pellon 805 Wonder-Under transfer web (17 in/43 cm wide) for twelve 7¼-by-3½-in/18.5-by-9-cm letters
- One 20-in/50-cm square pillow insert
- Coordinating thread for Front and Back
- Coordinating thread/s for appliquéd letters

FROM THE SEWING BASKET

- Water-soluble fabric marker
- Ruler
- Pen or pencil for tracing
- Pins
- Scissors for fabric

CUTTING

Fold the fabric in half, **right** sides together, and align the selvage edges. Using the fabric marker and the ruler, draw the dimensions below onto the **wrong** side of the fabric.

FROM FRONT AND BACK PILLOW FABRIC:

Cut one 21-by-10½-in/53-by-26.5-cm rectangle, on the fold.
Cut two 21-by-15½-in/53-by-39-cm rectangles. *(See fabric layout diagram.)*
See below for instructions on cutting out appliqué letters.

* FABRIC LAYOUT DIAGRAM *

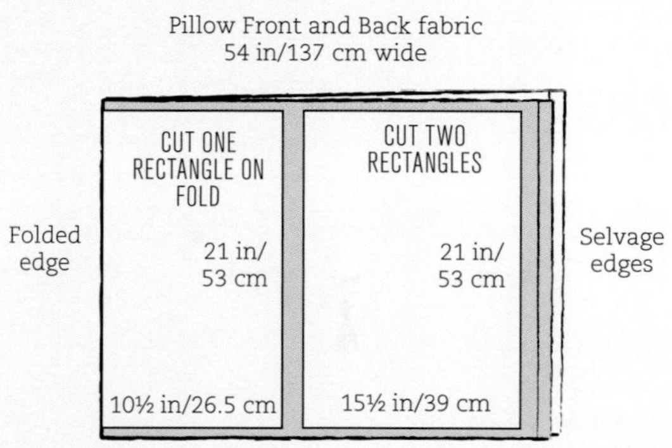

Pillow Front and Back fabric
54 in/137 cm wide

Folded edge	CUT ONE RECTANGLE ON FOLD	CUT TWO RECTANGLES	Selvage edges
	21 in/ 53 cm	21 in/ 53 cm	
	10½ in/26.5 cm	15½ in/39 cm	

ASSEMBLE

STEP 1: FRONT

A Download the free Headline font and print out the letters. You can also freehand draw your own letters or go online and choose a font you love and enlarge as necessary. The letters on our pillow are about 7¼ by 3½ in/18.5 by 9 cm.

B Trace the letters onto the transfer web. Depending on the type of transfer web you use, you may need to trace the letters backward so they appear the correct way when fused to the fabric. Roughly cut around each traced letter.

C Fuse the web to the **wrong** side of the fabric scraps, following the manufacturer's instructions. Carefully cut out the letters around the traced marks, keeping the paper side of the transfer web in place.

D   Position the letters onto the **right** side of the Front piece where you want them to be stitched down. Once you decide on the placement of each letter, peel off the paper side of the transfer web and fuse the **wrong** side of the letter to the **right** side of the Front piece, following the manufacturer's instructions.

E   Change the settings on your sewing machine to the zigzag stitch with a very short stitch length, so you can do a satin stitch *(see Glossary)* around each letter. On a scrap of fabric, test different zigzag width settings. When you find the width of the satin stitch you like, carefully stitch around each letter.

STEP 2: BACK AND FINISHING

A   With the Back pieces **wrong**-side up on your ironing board, fold a long raw edge over 1 in/2.5 cm and press. Then fold that same edge over another 1 in/2.5 cm and press again. Repeat on other Back piece. Pin the hems in place as needed. Edge stitch *(see Glossary)* along the inner folded edges of each Back piece.

B   Place the Front piece **right**-side up on a flat surface. Then place one of the Back pieces on top of the Front, **right** sides together. Align all raw edges and make sure that the Back hemmed edge is toward the center of the Front piece. Pin together. Repeat with second Back piece on the opposite side of the Front. The Back hemmed edges should overlap about 6 in/15 cm. *(See illustration.)*

C   Sew around the perimeter of the pillow cover with a ½-in/12-mm seam allowance. Pivot around each corner as you go. Clip the corners *(see Glossary)* and finish the raw edges in your preferred method.

D   Turn the Pillow cover **right**-side out through the overlap opening. Press flat, then topstitch *(see Glossary)* around the perimeter ¼ in/6 mm. Stuff with the pillow insert.

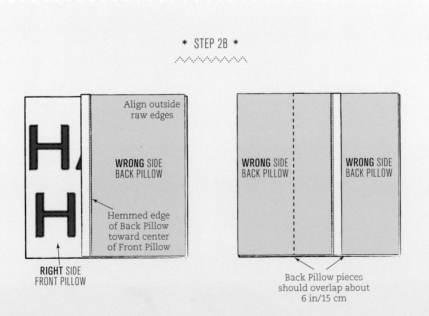

* STEP 2B *

Align outside raw edges

WRONG SIDE BACK PILLOW

Hemmed edge of Back Pillow toward center of Front Pillow

RIGHT SIDE FRONT PILLOW

WRONG SIDE BACK PILLOW

WRONG SIDE BACK PILLOW

Back Pillow pieces should overlap about 6 in/15 cm

4

Dorothy's Drapery

You don't need to spend a lot on pricey drapery—not when you can make it yourself. Each of our two finished curtains started out as two lengths of Sis Boom fabric seamed together and then lined. Add a bamboo pole and some bamboo rings to get that effortless tropical elegance.

NOTE: If you are using a large-scale print and want it to match at the seams, you will need to buy extra yardage. Please see page 17 for tips on how to figure this out.

Finished size of each curtain:

89 BY 80 IN/226 BY 203 CM

MATERIALS

- 11½ yd/10.5 m printed mid-weight cotton fabric (45 in/114 cm wide) for Curtain
- 11½ yd/10.5 m solid white drapery lining fabric (54 in/137 cm wide) for Lining
- 5 yd/4.5 m Deep Pleat Tape by Drapery Sewing Supplies
- 16 long-neck 4-prong pleat hooks
- 16 drapery rings to fit your curtain rod
- Coordinating thread

FROM THE SEWING BASKET

- Scissors for fabric
- Pins
- Water-soluble fabric marker or chalk pencil
- Ruler
- Hand sewing needle

CUTTING

Cut the Curtain fabric in half so you have two 5¾-yd/5.25-m-long pieces. Repeat with the Lining fabric. Fold each fabric in half, with **right** sides together, and align the cut edges. Using the fabric marker and the ruler, draw the dimensions below onto the **wrong** side of the fabric.

FROM CURTAIN FABRIC:

Cut four 95½-by-42 ½-in/243-by-108-cm rectangles.

FROM LINING FABRIC:

Cut four 94½-by-41-in/240 by 104-cm rectangles.
  (See fabric layout diagram.)

ASSEMBLE

STEP 1: SEAM CURTAIN AND LINING PANELS

A   Place 2 Curtain panels **right** sides together, align all raw edges, and pin along 1 long edge. Sew together with a ½-in/12-mm seam allowance. Press the seam open and finish the raw edges in your preferred method. Repeat with the other Curtain panels.

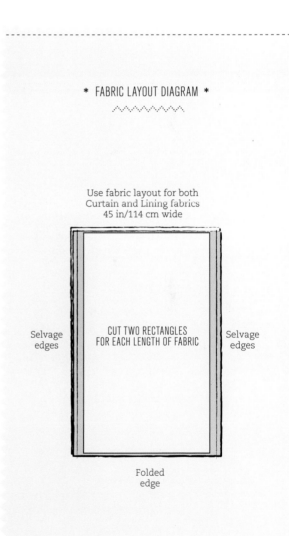

* FABRIC LAYOUT DIAGRAM *

Use fabric layout for both Curtain and Lining fabrics 45 in/114 cm wide

Selvage edges

CUT TWO RECTANGLES FOR EACH LENGTH OF FABRIC

Selvage edges

Folded edge

B   Repeat step 1A with the Lining panels.

C   With a Curtain **wrong**-side up, fold 1 short edge over 3 in/7.5 cm and press. Fold the same edge over another 3 in/7.5 cm and press, pinning as needed. Edge stitch along the inner folded edge. Repeat on the other Curtain and both Lining pieces.

STEP 2: JOIN CURTAIN AND LINING

A   Place 1 Curtain and 1 Lining piece with **right** sides together, align along 1 long side edge and along the top edge, then pin together along the side edge only. The Curtain panel will be 3 in/7.5 cm wider and 1 in/2.5 cm longer than the Lining. Sew the side edge together with a ½-in/12-mm seam allowance. Then pull the unsewn side of the Lining piece over to align with the other long side edge of the Curtain, and pin. Sew together with a ½-in/12-mm seam allowance. Press the seams open and finish the raw edges in your preferred method. Repeat with the other Curtain and Lining piece.

B   Keeping the joined Curtain and Lining pieces with **right** sides together, align along the top raw edges, making sure to match up the center seam. Since the Lining piece is narrower than the Curtain, the Curtain fabric will roll toward the Lining side about 1½ in/4 cm on each side. Pin the top edges and sew together with a ½-in/12-mm seam allowance. Trim off the corners and turn the joined panels **right**-side out. Press along the top edge and each side edge to set crease. Repeat with the other Curtain and Lining pieces. *(See illustration.)*

C   With a hand sewing needle and thread, slipstitch each bottom Curtain corner to hem. *(See illustration.)*

STEP 3: PLEAT TAPE AND HOOKS

A   With the Lining side of 1 Curtain face up, place the pleat tape ¼ in/6 mm from the top edge and pin in place. Make sure the "pocket" side of the pleat tape is **right**-side up. Turn the raw edges of the short end of the tape under so the fold lines up with the Lining/Curtain seam. Edge stitch the pleat tape in place along both top and bottom edges. Repeat with the other Curtain.

B   Working your way out from the center of a Curtain, count 7 pleat pockets. Place the first prong of a pleat hook into that pocket. Working toward the center, skip 3 pockets and place the second prong into next (fourth) pocket. From the second prong, skip 3 pockets and then place the third prong into next (fourth) pocket. From the third prong, skip 3 pockets and then place the fourth prong into next (fourth) pocket. You have now created your first set of pleats. Place the next set of pleats 10 or 11 pockets away from the first set. Working in the same manner, place the prong in the pocket, skip 3 pockets, and place next prong in next pocket. Do this along the entire top edge of the Curtain. Repeat on the second Curtain. If you are confused, the manufacturer has great instructions and videos on how to use the Deep Pleat Tape with the 4-prong pleat hooks.

C   Place drapery rings on your curtain rod. With the **right** side of the Curtain toward you, slip each hook into the small eyelet at the bottom of a drapery ring.

* STEP 2B *

* STEP 2B *

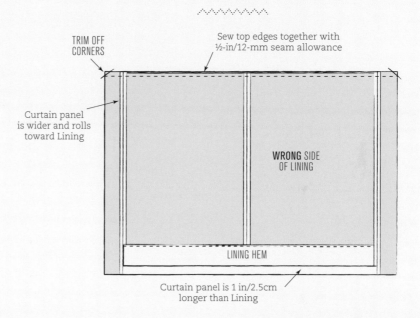

TRIM OFF CORNERS

Sew top edges together with
½-in/12-mm seam allowance

Curtain panel
is wider and rolls
toward Lining

WRONG SIDE
OF LINING

LINING HEM

Curtain panel is 1 in/2.5cm
longer than Lining

* STEP 2C *

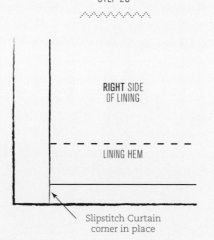

RIGHT SIDE
OF LINING

LINING HEM

Slipstitch Curtain
corner in place

Accessorize

№

5

PRETTY
BOX

№
6
EVERYTHING
IS COMING UP
ROSES BASKET

Pretty Box

CONTRIBUTED BY *Janis Bullis*

I love pretty things, and this box makes getting organized seem like fun. It's ideal for holding sewing notions, photo collections, correspondence, and bibs and bobs. This is a very simple project—you could whip up a few boxes in an afternoon. Once the glue dries, don't delay! Put this useful box right to work.

Finished size:

VARIES, DEPENDING ON BOX

MATERIALS

- Sturdy box of your choice with a separate or attached lid
- Enough fabric to cover box and lid *(see below)*
- Pins
- Spray adhesive
- Tracing paper
- Clothespins

FROM THE CRAFT CABINET

- Flexible tape measure
- Ruler
- Pencil
- Scissors for paper and fabric
- White glue
- Drop cloth or newspaper to protect your work surface

MEASURE AND DRAW PATTERN

With the tape measure, take the measurements of your box and write them down. Use these measurements to draw your pattern on the tracing paper, with pencil and ruler. Use the diagrams on the next page for taking the measurements and the drawing pattern. *(See illustration.)*

CUTTING

Cut out the pattern/s from the tracing paper. Lay the pattern/s on the fabric, pin in place, and cut out 1 piece for each box component you need.

ASSEMBLE

STEP 1: APPLY FABRIC

A   When applying spray adhesive, work in a well-ventilated area, and protect your work surface with a drop cloth or newspaper. Place the fabric **wrong**-side up and spray with adhesive, making sure to follow the manufacturer's instructions. Spray each piece just before using.

B   For a box with a separate lid, center the box on the fabric, making sure to smooth out any wrinkles. Then gently wrap the fabric over 1 side of the box. At the corners, wrap the raw edges around to the other sides. Wrap the excess fabric over the top edge into the inside of the box. Repeat on the opposite side of the box. On the 2 remaining sides, fold under the raw edges at the corners, then wrap the fabric up and over the top edge and into the inside of the box. If necessary, use a bit of white glue at the inside corners or on any loose edges. Repeat on the lid, then add the lining piece to the inside of the lid. You can use clothespins along the edges of the box to hold the fabric in place until the glue dries.

C For a box with an attached lid, center the fabric along the front and sides, and wrap the raw edges to the inside and bottom of the box. Center the bottom of the box on the bottom/back/top piece, wrapping the fabric around the back and up over the top. Fold over any excess fabric at the top to the inside. Trim off any excess fabric at the back and side edges. Center the lid lining piece on the inside of the lid. You can use clothespins along the edges of the box to hold the fabric in place until the glue dries.

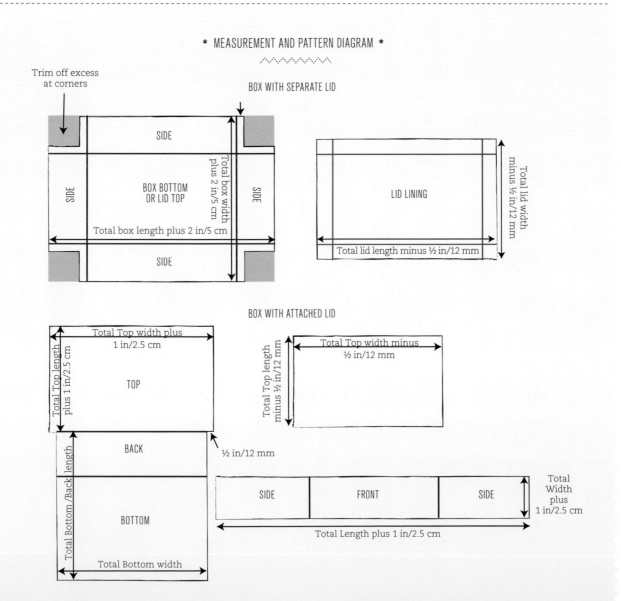

* MEASUREMENT AND PATTERN DIAGRAM *

Everything is Coming Up Roses Basket

Nothing delights more than a basket full of posies! This project turns the basket inside out by putting the flowers on the outside. The large basket takes an enormous amount of flowers, so it's best to buy dime-store flowers to mix in with the more pricey vintage ones. You can create a cheerful multicolored basket, like the one here, or a more subtle monochromatic one. Make it even more lush by adding satin or velvet ribbon with the flowers.

NOTE: Flower sizes should vary, but a good rule of thumb is to use smaller flowers on smaller baskets and the larger ones on big baskets.

Finished size:

VARIES, DEPENDING ON THE BASKET

MATERIALS

- 1 basket
- 100 to 400 artificial flowers, new and vintage, depending on size of basket and size of flower heads
- Various lengths and colors of satin or velvet ribbon (optional)

FROM THE CRAFT CABINET

Hot glue gun and glue sticks

ASSEMBLE

STEP 1: FLOWERS

A   Remove the flower heads from the stems of the flowers. Discard the stems and leaves.

B   Start at the top edge of the basket and glue the flower heads in place. Place the flowers very close together and work your way around the entire top edge. If you are using ribbon, glue it to the basket along with the flowers, either by tying the ribbon into bows and placing it next to a flower or by weaving the ribbon around the flower heads. Continue to glue the flower heads around the basket, working from top to bottom, until the entire basket is completely covered. If you have extra flower heads, you can glue them to the very top inside edge of the basket so they wrap over the top. Let the glue dry completely before using the basket.

Millie's Market Tote

CONTRIBUTED BY *Tammy Gilley*

This roomy tote will easily hold your farmers' market purchases and keep your personal items nicely organized in the interior pockets. Depending on your fabric and handle choices, you can make this into a classy tote or go for a fun, girly vibe. We couldn't resist adding a big ol' silk flower pin for that Sis Boom touch.

Finished size (not including handles):

17-IN/43-CM WIDE BY 14-IN/35.5-CM TALL
BY 4-IN/10-CM DEEP

MATERIALS

- 1 yd/1 m printed mid-weight cotton fabric
  (45 in/114 cm wide) for Exterior
- 1¼ yd/1.2 m coordinating mid-weight cotton fabric
  (45 in/114 cm wide) for Lining
- 1½ yd/1.4 m Pellon Peltex 71F (fusible on one side) or
  similar extra-heavy fusible interfacing stabilizer
- 1 set Clover bamboo or amber purse handles
- Coordinating thread
- One 7-in/18-cm-diameter silk artificial flower (optional)
- One 1¼-in/3.2-cm-long pin back (optional)
- One 2½-in/6-cm felt circle (optional)

FROM THE SEWING BASKET

- Scissors for fabric
- Pins
- Water-soluble fabric marker or chalk pencil
- Ruler
- Turning tool

FROM THE CRAFT CABINET

- Hot glue gun and glue sticks if making flower pin

CUTTING

Fold the fabrics in half, **right** sides together, and align the
selvage edges. Using the fabric marker and the ruler, draw
the dimensions below onto the **wrong** sides of the fabrics.

FROM EXTERIOR TOTE FABRIC:

Cut two 15-by-18-in/38-by-46-cm rectangles, for Main panels.
Cut two 15-by-5 in/38-by-12-cm rectangles, for Side panels.
Cut one 5-by-9 in/12-by-23-cm rectangle, on the fold, for
   Bottom panel.
Cut four 2½-by-2-in/6-by-5-cm rectangles, for Handle Loops.
Cut one 2¼-by-22-in/5.5-by-56-cm strip, on the fold, for Binding.

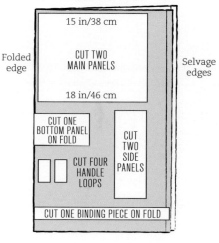

* FABRIC LAYOUT DIAGRAM *

Exterior fabric
45 in/114 cm wide

- 15 in/38 cm
- CUT TWO MAIN PANELS
- 18 in/46 cm
- Folded edge
- Selvage edges
- CUT ONE BOTTOM PANEL ON FOLD
- CUT TWO SIDE PANELS
- CUT FOUR HANDLE LOOPS
- CUT ONE BINDING PIECE ON FOLD

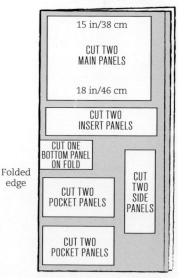

Lining fabric
45 in/114 cm wide

- 15 in/38 cm
- CUT TWO MAIN PANELS
- 18 in/46 cm
- CUT TWO INSERT PANELS
- CUT ONE BOTTOM PANEL ON FOLD
- Folded edge
- Selvage edges
- CUT TWO POCKET PANELS
- CUT TWO SIDE PANELS
- CUT TWO POCKET PANELS

FROM LINING FABRIC:

Cut two 15-by-18 in/38-by-46-cm rectangles, for Main lining.
Cut two 15-by-5-in/38-by-12-cm rectangles, for Side lining.
Cut one 5-by-9-in/12-by-23-cm rectangle, on the fold, for Bottom lining.
Cut two 5-by-18-in/12-by-46-cm rectangles, for Bottom Insert panels.
Cut four 7½-by-12½-in/19-by-32-cm rectangles, for interior Pockets.
(See fabric layout diagram.)

FROM PELLON PELTEX:

Cut two 14½-by-17-in/37-by-43-cm rectangles, for Main interfacing.
Cut two 14½-by-4-in/37-by-10-cm rectangles, for Side interfacing.
Cut one 4-by-17-in/10-by-43-cm rectangle, for Bottom interfacing.
Cut one 3¾-by-16¾-in/9.5-by-42.5-cm rectangle, for Bottom Insert interfacing.

ASSEMBLE

STEP 1: APPLY INTERFACING, AND PRESS HANDLE LOOPS AND BINDING

A   Fuse the Peltex pieces to the **wrong** sides of the exterior Main, Side, and Bottom panels, following the manufacturer's instructions. You will want to align the top edges of the Front, Back, and Side panels with the top edges of the Peltex, leaving ½ in/12 mm of exterior fabric visible along 3 edges. For the Bottom panel, center the Peltex on the fabric, leaving ½ in/12 mm of exterior fabric visible on all 4 sides. *(See illustration.)*

B   With **wrong** sides together, fold over and press 1 short end of the Binding strip ½ in/12 mm.

C   Fold and press the 4 Handle Loops and Binding, following the pressing instructions to make a double-fold binding. *(See page 20.)*

D   Sew closed the 2 folded edges on the Handle Loops, ⅛ in/3 mm from the edge. Then topstitch ⅛ in/3 mm from the edge on the opposite side of the Handle Loops. You should end up with four 2½-by-½-in/6-cm-by-12-mm strips.

STEP 2: EXTERIOR

A   Align the raw side edges of 1 Main panel and 1 Side panel, with **right** sides together, and pin. Sew together with a ½-in/12-mm seam allowance, stopping ½ in/12 mm from the bottom edge (where the interfacing ends). Repeat on the opposite side of the Main panel with the other Side panel, and then sew the other Main Panel to each of the Side panels. It is important to leave ½ in/12 mm at the bottom of each seam unstitched. *(See illustration.)*

B   Place 1 long edge of the Bottom panel and the bottom edge of 1 Main panel **right** sides together, aligning the raw edges, and pin in place. Sew together with ½-in/12-mm seam allowance, starting and stopping the stitching ½ in/12 mm from each end of the Bottom panel. *(See illustration.)*

C   Repeat step 2B on 1 of the Side panels and 1 short end of the Bottom panel.

✳ STEP 1A: PELTEX PLACEMENT ✳

Align Peltex to top edges of Main and Side Panels, leaving ½ in/12 mm of **wrong** side of Exterior fabric exposed on the other edges

Center Peltex on Bottom Panel, leaving ½ in/12mm of **wrong** side Exterior fabric exposed on all edges

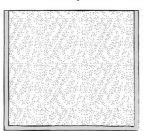

✳ STEPS 2A & 2B ✳

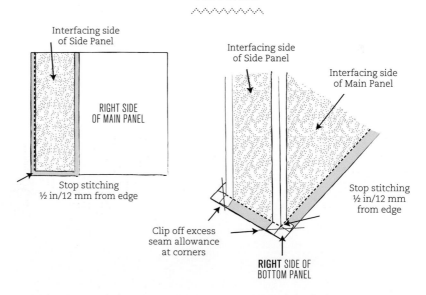

Interfacing side of Side Panel

RIGHT SIDE OF MAIN PANEL

Stop stitching ½ in/12 mm from edge

Interfacing side of Side Panel

Interfacing side of Main Panel

Stop stitching ½ in/12 mm from edge

Clip off excess seam allowance at corners

RIGHT SIDE OF BOTTOM PANEL

D   Repeat steps 2B and 2C to sew the last 2 Bottom panel edges to the remaining Main and Side panel edges.

E   Trim off the corners of the Bottom panel, making sure not to cut the stitching. Turn the exterior of the tote **right**-side out and gently push the corners out with a turning tool.

STEP 3: LINING AND POCKET

A   Place 2 interior Pocket pieces **right** sides together, aligning all raw edges, and pin. Sew 3 of the sides together with a ½-in/12-mm seam allowance, leaving 1 long edge open. Clip the corners and turn the Pocket **right**-side out. Fold the bottom raw edges up ½ in/12 mm. This side is now the **wrong** side of the Pocket. Repeat with the second set of Pocket pieces.

B   Fold both Main lining panels in half, aligning the short ends, and gently crease the center with a finger. Repeat with the interior Pocket pieces.

C   With **right** sides up, align the center creases of 1 Main lining panel and 1 Pocket, placing the Pocket 3½ in/9 cm from the top edge of the Main lining panel. Pin the Pocket to the Main lining panel, making sure it is straight. Sew 3 sides of the Pocket to the Main lining panel, ⅛ in/3 mm from the Pocket edge, making sure to leave the top edge open. If you like, you can stitch along the center crease of the Pocket to create 2 compartments. Repeat with the other Main lining panel and Pocket. *(See illustration.)*

D   Follow steps 2A through 2E to sew the lining.

E   Place both Bottom Insert pieces **right** sides together, aligning all edges, and pin. Sew 3 edges together with a ½-in/12-mm seam allowance, leaving 1 short end open. Clip the corners and turn the Bottom Insert **right**-side out. Slip the Bottom Insert interfacing into the Bottom Insert. Press both raw edges of fabric under ½ in/12 mm and edge stitch the short end closed.

STEP 4: FINISHING

A   Place the lining inside the tote with **wrong** sides together and align along the top raw edges, making sure that all the side seams match. Pin in place.

B   At the top edge on the **right** side of the Main lining panel, use the fabric marker to designate where Handle Loops should be placed. The Handle Loops should be centered on the main lining panel's top edge. Slip 1 short end of a Handle Loop through the Handle opening, and align the raw edges of the Handle Loop with the top raw edge of the bag on the lining side. Pin the folded Handle Loop in place through all layers. Repeat on other side of the same handle. Baste the Handle Loops in place ⅜ in/1 cm from top edge through all layers. Repeat on the other Main lining panel. *(See illustration.)*

C   With **right** sides together, place the short folded end of the Binding strip at the center of 1 Main lining panel. Unfold and align the long raw edge of the Binding with the top raw edge of the tote, and pin together around entire top edge, taking the pins out from step 4A as you go. Overlap the short raw end of the Binding over the folded short end, and pin. Sew the Binding to the top edge of the tote with a ½-in/12-mm seam allowance, making sure to catch the Handle Loops in this seam.

D   Fold the Binding over the top edge, toward the exterior of the tote, enclosing all raw edges. Pin the Binding in place, making sure to cover the stitching from step 4C. Carefully edge stitch along the inside folded edge of the Binding. Place the Bottom Insert inside your tote, and you're ready to go.

STEP 5: OPTIONAL FLOWER

A   Measure the distance between the latch and the hinge of the pin back. Mark this distance, centered, on the felt circle with a fabric marker. Cut a small slit at each of these marks. Put the latch and the hinge through the slits. When you look at the felt circle, the base of the pin will be hidden behind the felt.

B   Remove the stem and any bulky plastic from the back of your flower, while keeping the flower head intact. Glue the felt circle with pin back to the center back of the flower. Let dry completely and then pin onto your tote.

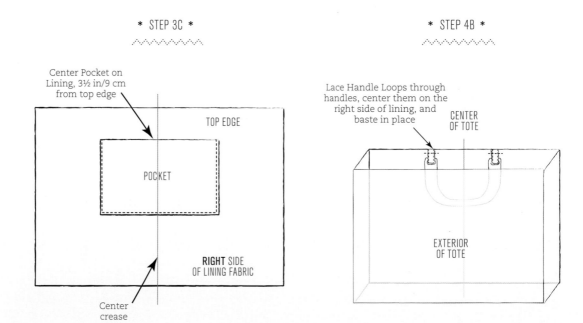

* STEP 3C *

Center Pocket on Lining, 3½ in/9 cm from top edge

TOP EDGE

POCKET

RIGHT SIDE OF LINING FABRIC

Center crease

* STEP 4B *

Lace Handle Loops through handles, center them on the right side of lining, and baste in place

CENTER OF TOTE

EXTERIOR OF TOTE

Laundry Bag

No more humdrum laundry: This bag will cheer up the most mundane of chores. The bag looks great hanging on a hook in a laundry room or behind a bedroom door. Make a couple of bags, one for lights and one for darks. The bag would also make a lovely gift for someone who travels a lot, to use in place of a plastic bag.

Finished size:

26 BY 20 IN/66 BY 50 CM

MATERIALS

- ⅝ yd/57 cm printed mid-weight cotton fabric (45 in/114 cm wide) for Top
- ¼ yd/23 cm coordinating mid-weight cotton fabric (45 in/114 cm wide) for Middle and Tie
- ¼ yd/23 cm coordinating mid-weight cotton fabric (45 in/114 cm wide) for Bottom
- ⅞ yd/80 cm light- to mid-weight cotton canvas fabric (45 in/114 cm wide) for Lining
- Coordinating thread

FROM THE SEWING BASKET

- Scissors for fabric
- Ruler
- Water-soluble fabric marker
- Pins
- Safety pin

CUTTING

Fold all fabrics in half, **right** sides together, and align the selvage edges. Using the fabric marker and the ruler, draw the dimensions below onto the **wrong** side of the fabrics.

FROM TOP FABRIC:

Cut one 19-by-20½-in/48-by-52-cm rectangle, on the fold.

With the ruler and the marker, make 2 marks along the 19-in/48-cm raw edge: Make 1 mark 3½ in/9 cm from the top edge, then another mark 1 in/2.5 cm below the first. (See illustration.)

Clip small notches, through both layers, into the seam allowance at these marks.

FROM MIDDLE AND TIE FABRIC:

Cut one 4-by-20½-in/10-by-52-cm rectangle, on the fold, for Middle piece.

Cut two 2-by-20½-in/5-by-52-cm rectangles, on the fold, for Tie pieces.

FROM BOTTOM FABRIC:

Cut one 8-by-20½-in/20-by-52-cm rectangle, on the fold.

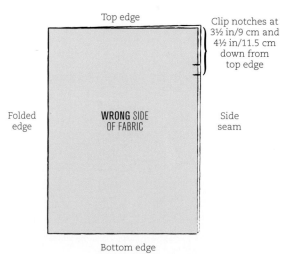

* SKETCH FOR LAUNDRY BAG NOTCHING *

Bag piece folded in half widthwise

Top edge

Clip notches at 3½ in/9 cm and 4½ in/11.5 cm down from top edge

Folded edge

WRONG SIDE OF FABRIC

Side seam

Bottom edge

Top fabric
45 in/114 cm wide

CUT ONE
RECTANGLE
ON FOLD

Folded
edge

Selvage
edges

Middle/Tie fabric
45 in/114 cm wide

Folded
edge

Selvage
edges

CUT THREE
RECTANGLES ON FOLD

Bottom fabric
45 in/114 cm wide

Folded
edge

Selvage
edges

CUT ONE
RECTANGLE ON FOLD

Lining fabric
45 in/114 cm wide

CUT ONE
RECTANGLE
ON FOLD

Folded
edge

Selvage
edges

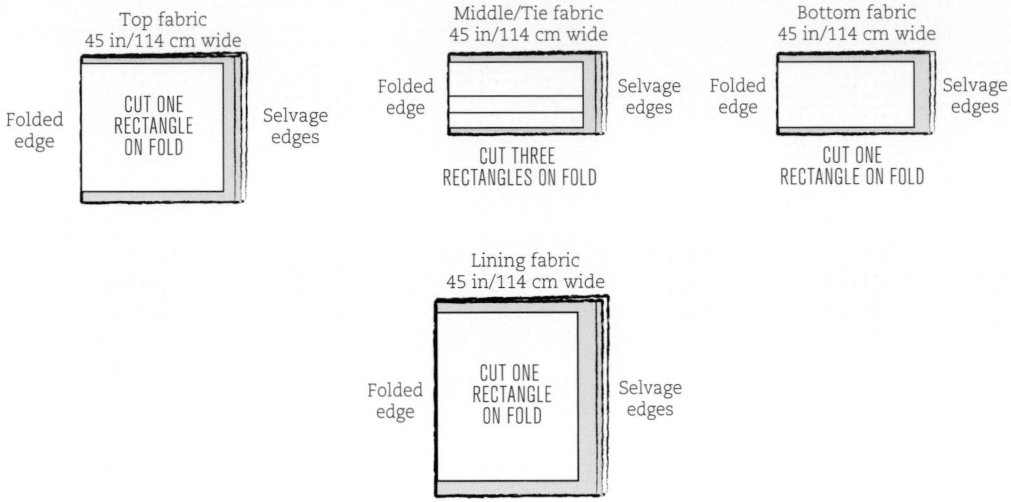

FROM LINING FABRIC:

Cut one 26½-by-20½-in/67-by-52-cm rectangle, on the fold. *(See fabric layout diagram.)*

ASSEMBLE

STEP 1: SEW TOP, MIDDLE, BOTTOM, AND LINING

A   With **right** sides together, align the raw edges of the Top and Middle pieces along one long edge and pin. Make sure not to align the top edge of the Top piece; the top edge is the edge closest to the notches. Sew together with a ½-in/12-mm seam allowance. Press the seam open.

B   Follow step 1A to join the Bottom piece to the Middle piece.

C   Fold the Lining piece in half widthwise, with **right** sides together, and align the long raw edges. Pin the 2 sides together, leaving the upper edge open. Sew the pinned edges together with a ½-in/12-mm seam allowance, and pivot at the corner. Trim off the bottom corners and press the seams open.

STEP 2: JOIN BAG AND LINING

A   Fold the joined Bag piece in half widthwise, with **right** sides together, and align the long raw edges. Pin the 2 sides together, leaving the upper edge open. Beginning at the bottom of the Bag, sew a seam with a ½-in/12-mm seam allowance. Pivot at the corner and continue up the side to the first set of notches; backstitch to end the seam. Move the fabric and begin sewing at the second set of notches, then continue sewing to the upper edge, leaving a 1-in/2.5-cm opening in the side seam between the notches. *(See illustration.)* Clip off the bottom corners and press the seams open.

B Sew the seam allowances flat at the side seam opening by topstitching *(see Glossary)* ⅛ in/3 mm from each folded edge. *(See illustration.)*

C To prepare the casing, with the Bag inside out, fold the upper edge over ½ in/12 mm and press. Fold over and press the top edge again 2 in/5 cm from the first fold.

D With the Bag inside out and the Lining **right**-side out, slip the Lining onto the Bag. Unfold the top edge of the Bag, and align the top edge of the Lining to the second fold from the top edge of the Bag. Make sure to match both pieces at the side seam. Fold the top edge of the Bag over the Lining and pin together along the inner folded edge. Edge stitch *(see page 21)* along the inner folded edge. With the water-soluble fabric marker, draw a straight line around the bag, 1 in/ 2.5 cm up from the stitched edge; stitch along this line to create the Tie casing. Turn the Bag **right**-side out, then carefully push out the corners and press.

STEP 3: FINISHING

A Arrange the Tie pieces **right** sides together, and align along 1 short end and pin. Sew together with a ½-in/12-mm seam allowance. Press the seam open. Follow the pressing instructions for double-fold binding *(see page 20)* to press the long Tie strip.

B Pin the 2 long folded edges of the Tie strip together and topstitch closed ⅛ in/3 mm from the edge. On the opposite edge of the Tie, topstitch ⅛ in/3 mm to complete the Tie.

C Place a safety pin in 1 end of the Tie and thread it through the Bag casing. Align the Tie ends and knot them together.

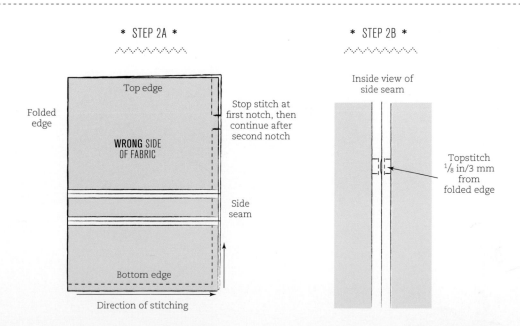

* STEP 2A *

Top edge

Folded edge

WRONG SIDE OF FABRIC

Stop stitch at first notch, then continue after second notch

Side seam

Bottom edge

Direction of stitching

* STEP 2B *

Inside view of side seam

Topstitch ⅛ in/3 mm from folded edge

Jimbo Jumbo Dog Bed Cover

Every member of the family deserves a bit of pampering, even the dog. My dog George is a big Labradoodle, and I had a hard time finding an attractive cover large enough for his bed. I then came up with the idea to cover his bed with a simple patchwork quilt, and now everyone is happy. He likes the bed so much that it was difficult to keep the cover clean for the photo shoot! This is a project where you can use any fabric scraps you have laying around.

NOTE: Since this cover will get a lot of use and needs to be washable, simple quilting stitches will work best (diagonal lines, meandering free motion, or stitch in the ditch). You don't want to spend time doing delicate hand quilting or tying by hand. We have also given you two options: a quilted top with a quilted bottom or a quilted top with a canvas bottom.

NOTE: The size of the dog bed used for the photo is no longer available, so we had to slightly resize the cover to accommodate a more standard 45 by 30 in/ 114 by 76 cm bed. We also added a seam at the bottom for easier assembly.

Finished size:

46 BY 31 BY 4 IN/117 BY 79 BY 10 CM

MATERIALS

FOR QUILTED TOP AND BOTTOM OPTION:

- Seven ½-yd/45-cm lengths of different printed mid-weight cotton fabrics (45 in/114 cm wide) for pieced Top and Bottom
  OR
- Seventy 8½-in/21.5-cm random fabric squares for pieced Top and Bottom
- 3½ yd/3.25 m mid-weight cotton fabric (45 in/114 cm wide) for Backing
- 3½ yd/3.25 m cotton batting (45 in/114 cm wide)
- One 26-in/66-cm coordinating zipper
- One 45-by-30-in/114–by-76-cm dog bed
- Coordinating thread

FOR QUILTED TOP AND CANVAS BOTTOM OPTION:

- Seven ¼-yd/23-cm lengths of 7 different printed mid-weight cotton fabrics (45 in/114 cm wide) for pieced Top
  OR
- Thirty-five 8½-in/21.5-cm random fabric squares for pieced Top
- 1¾ yd/1.6 m mid-weight cotton fabric (45 in/114 cm wide) for Backing
- 1½ yd/1.4 m mid-weight cotton duck canvas fabric (54 in/137 cm wide) for Bottom
- 1¾ yd/1.6 m cotton batting (45 in/114 cm wide, or crib size)
- One 26-in/66-cm coordinating zipper
- One 45-by-30-in/114-by-76-cm dog bed
- Coordinating thread

FROM THE SEWING BASKET

- Scissors for fabric
- Rotary cutter and cutting mat (optional, but makes cutting all those squares a lot easier)
- Clear ruler
- Pins
- Water-soluble fabric marker
- Safety pins (optional)
- Zipper foot for your sewing machine
- Darning foot for your sewing machine (for free-motion quilting option)
- Walking foot for your sewing machine (for any other machine quilting option)

FROM THE CRAFT CABINET

- Masking tape
- Quilt basting spray (temporary fabric adhesive)

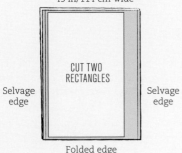

* FABRIC LAYOUT DIAGRAM *

QUILTED TOP AND BOTTOM OPTION:

For each Quilt Top fabric
45 in/114 cm wide

Selvage edge | CUT TEN SQUARES | Selvage edge

For Backing fabric and Batting
45 in/114 cm wide

Selvage edge | CUT TWO RECTANGLES | Selvage edge

Folded edge

QUILTED TOP ONLY OPTION:

For Backing fabric and Batting
45 in/114 cm wide

Selvage edge | CUT ONE RECTANGLE | Selvage edge

For each Quilt Top fabric
45 in/114 cm wide

Selvage edge | CUT FIVE SQUARES | Selvage edge

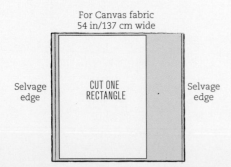

For Canvas fabric
54 in/137 cm wide

Selvage edge | CUT ONE RECTANGLE | Selvage edge

CUTTING

FOR QUILTED TOP AND BOTTOM OPTION:

FROM PIECED TOP AND BOTTOM FABRICS:
Cut seventy 8½-in/21.5-cm squares.

FROM BACKING FABRIC:
Cut two 60-by-44-in/152-by-112-cm rectangles.

FROM BATTING FABRIC:
Cut two 60-by-44-in/152-by-112-cm rectangles.

FOR QUILTED TOP AND CANVAS BOTTOM OPTION:

FROM PIECED TOP FABRICS:
Cut thirty-five 8½-in/21.5-cm squares.

FROM BACKING FABRIC:
Cut one 60-by-44-in/152-by-112-cm rectangle.

FROM BATTING FABRIC:
Cut one 60-by-44-in/152-by-112-cm rectangle.

FROM CANVAS:
Cut one 51-by-36-in/130-by-91-cm rectangle.
(See fabric layout diagram.)

ASSEMBLE

STEP 1: PIECE QUILT

A   For each quilted side of the cover, randomly lay out 35 squares in a grid of 5 squares by 7 squares.

B   Starting with the top horizontal row, pin and sew all the squares, with **right** sides together, using a ¼-in/6-mm seam allowance. Press the seam allowances to the left. Return the completed strip of squares to the layout.

C   Sew the second horizontal row of squares, with **right** sides together, using a ¼-in/6-mm seam allowance. Press all the seam allowances to the right. Return the completed strip to the layout.

D   Repeat steps 1B and 1C until you have all the squares sewn into 7 horizontal strips of 5 squares each, making sure that the seam allowances are pressed in alternating directions (left, right, left, and so on). This will help reduce bulk and interlock the strips when they are sewn together. *(See illustration.)*

E   Pin the first 2 strips, **right** sides together, carefully matching each vertical seam between each square. Sew together with a ¼-in/6-mm seam allowance. Press the seam down, toward the lower strip. Repeat until all 7 strips are sewn together.

F   Repeat steps 1B to 1E if making the quilted Bottom.

STEP 2: PREP FOR QUILTING

A   Lay the Backing piece flat on the floor, **right**-side down, and tape the edges to floor with masking tape. Lay the Batting on top of the Backing. Smooth out any wrinkles, and then place the pieced quilt Top, **right**-side up, centered on the Batting. Smooth out any wrinkles. The Top will be about 2 in/5 cm smaller on all sides than the Batting and Backing.

B   Fold back the Batting and Top so the upper half of the **wrong** side of the Backing is visible. Spray the Backing and Batting lightly with basting spray. Gradually roll the Batting into place over the Backing. Smooth out any wrinkles as necessary. Then lightly spray the Batting and the **wrong** side of the Top with basting spray. Gradually roll the Top into place over the Batting. Smooth out any wrinkles. Repeat for the lower half of the quilt. These 3 layers are now called the quilt sandwich.

C   Starting from the center of the quilt sandwich and working your way to the edges, use safety pins to attach all 3 layers together.

D   Repeat steps 2A to 2C if making the quilted Bottom.

STEP 3: QUILT AND CUT

A   Quilt the sandwiched layers together using your preferred method.

B   With the fabric marker and the ruler, draw a 51-by-36-in/130-by-91-cm rectangle centered on the Top. *(See illustration.)* Cut off the excess Top, Batting, and Backing, making sure that the corners are square and the edges are straight.

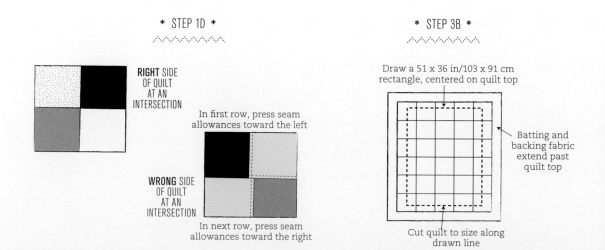

* STEP 1D *

RIGHT SIDE
OF QUILT
AT AN
INTERSECTION

In first row, press seam
allowances toward the left

WRONG SIDE
OF QUILT
AT AN
INTERSECTION

In next row, press seam
allowances toward the right

* STEP 3B *

Draw a 51 x 36 in/103 x 91 cm
rectangle, centered on quilt top

Batting and
backing fabric
extend past
quilt top

Cut quilt to size along
drawn line

STEP 4A

Sew seam with regular stitch length to notch and backstitch

Notch 5 in/12 cm from each edge

Backstitch at notch and continue to sew seam with regular stitch length to end

Baste seam between notches

RIGHT SIDE OF BACKING FABRIC WRONG SIDE OF COVER

Center zipper on seam between notches, sew zipper in place, ¼ in/6 mm from edge of tape and seam allowance

Direction of sewing

Press seam open

STEP 4C

Side seam

BACKING SIDE OF QUILTED COVER

Draw a straight line across point at gusset notches

Bottom seam

Sew along marked line

C   Repeat steps 3A and 3B if making the quilted Bottom.

D   Finish the raw edges of the Top and Bottom with a zigzag stitch or a serger.

STEP 4: FINISHING

A   Put the zipper foot on your sewing machine. Place the Top and Bottom of the cover with **right** sides together, align all raw edges, and pin together along one of the short sides. Measure 5 in/ 12 cm from each side, and clip notches into the seam allowance of the pinned side. Starting at 1 end, sew the pinned side to the first notch, with a ½-in/12-mm seam allowance, then backstitch. Don't remove the fabric from the sewing machine, and keep the seam allowance even. Change the stitch length to baste, then baste to the second notch and stop. Change the stitch length back to the normal setting, backstitch, and continue sewing to the end. Unfold the joined pieces so they are in a single layer and press the seam open. Center the zipper **right**-side down over the basted seam, between the notches, and pin in place. Starting at the top of 1 side of the zipper, sew through all layers, ¼ in/6 mm from the edge of the zipper tape and seam allowance. Sewing in the opposite direction, sew the other side of the zipper tape as above. Remove the basting stitches and open the zipper. *(See illustration.)*

B   Place the Top and Bottom of the cover with **right** sides together, align the 3 raw edges, and pin. Sew together with a ½-in/12-mm seam allowance, pivoting at each corner. Trim off the corners, and press the seams open.

C   To create gussets, fold one side seam down to meet and match up with the bottom seam. This will form a triangle. With the ruler and fabric marker, draw a straight line perpendicular to the side seam 2 in/5 cm from the tip of the triangle. This line should measure about 4 in/10 cm. Pin and sew along the line. Clip off the triangle, leaving a ½-in/12-mm seam allowance. Repeat on the other 3 corners. *(See illustration.)*

D   Turn the cover **right**-side out through the zipper opening, and insert dog bed.

The Broad Brim

Whether you are gardening, grilling, playing with the kids, or frolicking at the beach, this is the chapeau for you. You will want to make a different one to match each of your outdoor activities. Wear it with the brim folded up or down; either way, this hat will have you covered. It is also the perfect accessory to make as a gift.

Finished sizes:

GIRLS' SIZE ADJUSTABLE TO FIT HEAD CIRCUMFERENCES
OF 19½ TO 22 IN/49.5 TO 56 CM

WOMEN'S SIZE ADJUSTABLE TO FIT HEAD CIRCUMFERENCE
OF 21½ TO 24 IN/54.5 TO 61 CM

MATERIALS

- ⅝ yd/57 cm printed mid-weight cotton fabric (45 in/114 cm wide) for Exterior
- ⅝ yd/57 cm coordinating mid-weight cotton fabric (45 in/114 cm wide) for Lining
- ½ yd/45 cm coordinating mid-weight cotton fabric (45 in/114 cm wide) for Binding, Band, and Casing
- ⅝ yd/57 cm muslin fabric (45 in/114 cm wide) for interlining
- ½ yd/45 cm Pellon Craft Fuse 808 or similar mid-weight nonwoven fusible interfacing
- 1 yd/1 m Pellon Shape-Flex SF101 or similar mid-weight woven fusible interfacing
- One 36-to-40-in/91-to-102-cm shoelace
- Coordinating thread

FROM THE SEWING BASKET

- Tracing paper and pencil (optional)
- Water-soluble fabric marker
- Ruler
- Pins
- Scissors for fabric
- Safety pin

CUTTING

Cut out (or trace with the tracing paper and the pencil) the Top, Crown, and Brim pattern pieces provided in the front pocket of this book.

FROM EXTERIOR FABRIC:

Fold the fabric in half, **right** sides together, and align the selvage edges.
Cut 1 Crown piece on the fold, 1 Top piece, and 2 Brim pieces.

FROM LINING FABRIC:

Fold the fabric in half, **right** sides together, and align the selvage edges.
Cut 1 Crown piece on the fold, 1 Top piece, and 2 Brim pieces.

FROM MUSLIN FABRIC:

Fold the fabric in half, **right** sides together, and align the selvage edges.
Cut 1 Crown piece on the fold, 1 Top piece, and 2 Brim pieces.

---

* FABRIC LAYOUT DIAGRAM *

Use this layout for the
Exterior, Lining, and Muslin
fabric 45 in/114 cm wide

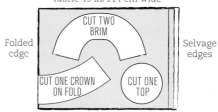

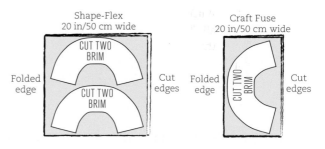

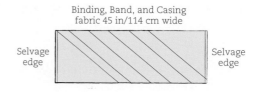

FROM PELLON CRAFT FUSE:

Fold the interfacing in half, and align along the short ends.
Cut 2 Brim pieces.

FROM PELLON SHAPE-FLEX:

Fold the interfacing in half, and align along the short ends.
Cut 4 Brim pieces.

FROM BINDING FABRIC:

With the fabric in a single layer:
Cut one 2¼-by-24-in/5.5-by-61-cm bias strip.
Cut enough 3-in-/7.5-cm-wide bias strips so that, when pieced together, they will measure at least
  80-in/203 cm. *(See fabric layout diagram.)*

ASSEMBLE

STEP 1: APPLY INTERLININGS

A   Fuse the Craft Fuse Brim pieces to 1 side of each muslin Brim piece, following the
      manufacturer's instructions.

B   Fuse the Shape-Flex Brim pieces to the **wrong** sides of the Exterior and Lining Brim pieces,
      following the manufacturer's instructions.

C   With **wrong** (interfaced) sides of the muslin Brim pieces and the Lining Brim pieces together, align
      all raw edges and pin. Along the smaller curved edge, baste the pieces together, ³/₈ in/1 cm from
      the edge. These will now be treated as a single piece and be referred to as the Brim Lining pieces.

D   Along the smaller curved edges of the Exterior Brim pieces, baste ³/₈ in/1 cm from the edge. This
      stitching is to help keep the curved edge from stretching.

E   Place the muslin Top piece on the **wrong** side of the Exterior Top piece, align the raw edges,
      and pin. Baste together ³/₈ in/1 cm from the edge. Place the muslin Crown piece on the **wrong**
      side of the Exterior Crown piece, align the raw edges, and pin. Along the smaller curved edge,
      baste together ³/₈ in/1 cm from the edge. These will now be treated as a single piece and be
      referred to as the Exterior pieces.

STEP 2: BINDING, BAND, AND CASING

A   Place the 2¼-by-24-in/5.5-by-61-cm bias strip **wrong**-side up, fold over one of the 2 long raw
      edges ½ in/12 mm, and press. This piece is the Crown Band piece.

B   Join the 3-in/7.5-cm bias strips together, following the instructions on *page* 20. Cut a 27-in-/
      69-cm-long piece off 1 end of the joined strip and set aside. Then fold and press the remaining
      joined bias strip into a double-fold binding *(see page 20.)*

C   Take the 27-in/69-cm piece of bias strip, fold 1 of the raw short ends over to the **wrong** side ¼ in/6 mm, and press. Then fold that edge over again ¼ in/6 mm, and press. Edge stitch along the inner folded edge. Then fold the entire strip in half lengthwise, and press. The other short end will be hemmed later. This piece is the inside Casing.

STEP 3: EXTERIOR PIECES

A   With **right**-sides up, align the raw edge of the Crown Band piece with the bottom raw edge of the Crown piece. Pin the Crown Band in place. Since the Crown piece is curved, you will have to stretch the bias-cut Crown Band piece slightly to fit and lay smoothly. Topstitch the top edge of the Crown Band piece to the Crown, ⅛ in/3 mm from the folded edge. Then baste the bottom raw edges together, ⅜ in/ 1 cm from the edge. Trim off any excess length of Crown Band piece. *(See illustration.)*

B   Fold the Exterior Crown piece in half, **wrong** sides together, align along the 2 short ends, and pin. Sew together with a ½-in/12-mm seam allowance. Press the seam open. Make small clips into the seam allowance, no more than ⅜ in/1 cm long, every 1 in/2.5 cm or so around the top edge (the smaller of the 2 edges) of the Crown piece. These clips will help the Crown piece fit together with the Top piece.

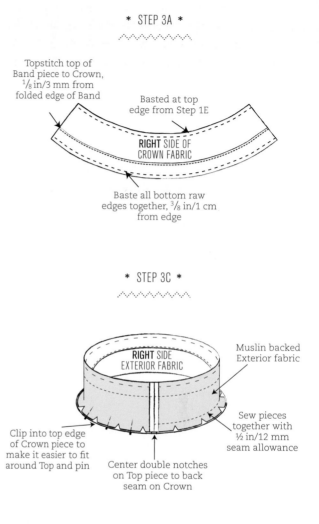

* STEP 3A *

Topstitch top of Band piece to Crown, ⅛ in/3 mm from folded edge of Band

Basted at top edge from Step 1E

RIGHT SIDE OF CROWN FABRIC

Baste all bottom raw edges together, ⅜ in/1 cm from edge

* STEP 3C *

Muslin backed Exterior fabric

RIGHT SIDE EXTERIOR FABRIC

Sew pieces together with ½ in/12 mm seam allowance

Clip into top edge of Crown piece to make it easier to fit around Top and pin

Center double notches on Top piece to back seam on Crown

C   With **right** sides together, center the double notches on the Top piece to the center back seam of the Crown piece, align the raw edges, and pin. Match the other 3 notches on the Top piece to the corresponding notches on the Crown piece in the same manner, pinning as you go. Align the raw edges of the Crown and Top pieces in between the notches, and pin as much as you feel necessary. If you are having a hard time fitting the pieces together, you many need to make a few more clips into the top edge seam allowance of the Crown piece. Once the pieces are aligned along the raw edges, sew together with a ½-in/12-mm seam allowance. Make small clips into the seam allowance of the Top piece every 1 in/2.5 cm or so, being careful not to cut into the seam. Turn the piece **right**-side out, and press the seam allowance toward the Crown. Topstitch around the top of the Crown ⅛ in/3 mm from the seam. *(See illustration.)*

D   With **right** sides together, align all edges of the 2 Brim pieces, and pin the 2 straight ends together. Sew together with a ½-in/12-mm seam allowance. Press both seams open.

E   With **right** sides together, match up the 2 side notches on the Exterior Crown piece to the 2 seams on the Exterior Brim, align the raw edges, and pin. Then match up the center back seam and center front notch on the Brim piece to the corresponding notches on the Brim, and pin together. Continue aligning the raw edges of the Crown and Brim pieces in between the notches, pinning as much as you feel necessary. If you are having a hard time fitting the pieces together, you may need to make some clips into the inside edge seam allowance of the Brim piece. Once the pieces are aligned along the raw edges, sew together with a ½-in/12-mm seam allowance. Make small clips into the seam allowance of the Crown piece every 1 in/2.5 cm or so, being careful not to cut into the seam. Press the seam toward the Crown, turn **right**-side out, and topstitch around the bottom Crown Band ⅛ in/3 mm from the seam, making sure to catch the seam allowance in the topstitching.

STEP 4: LINING AND CASING

A   Sew the Crown Lining center back seam following step 3B.

B   Sew the Crown Lining to the Top Lining following step 3C, omitting the topstitching around the Crown.

* STEP 4D *

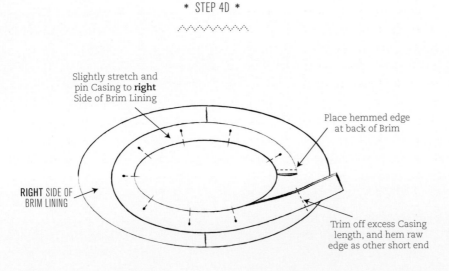

Slightly stretch and pin Casing to **right** Side of Brim Lining

Place hemmed edge at back of Brim

RIGHT SIDE OF BRIM LINING

Trim off excess Casing length, and hem raw edge as other short end

C Sew the Brim Lining pieces together following step 3D. Before pressing the seams open, trim off as much of the seam allowance as you can from the muslin piece only. Be careful not to cut into the seam. Then press the seams open.

D With **right** sides together, keeping the Casing folded in half, align the raw edges and pin the Casing around the inside edge of the Brim. You will want to start with the hemmed edge of the Casing. Pin it to the center back notch on the Brim, then continue pinning the Casing in place. You will need to gently stretch the Casing piece as you pin it to the Brim. Once you reach the center back notch on the Brim piece again, place a pin in the Casing only to mark where the 2 ends of the Casing meet. Don't remove this pin. Unpin the unhemmed end of the Casing from the Brim, a few inches/cm before reaching the center back notch. Trim off the excess Casing ½ in/12 mm from the pin. Hem this end of the Casing as you did in step 2C. Re-pin this end of the Casing to the Brim, and baste the Casing in place ⅜ in/1 cm from the edge. *(See illustration.)*

E Sew the Crown Lining to the Brim Lining following step 2E. Instead of pressing the seam allowance toward the Crown, press it toward the Brim. Then topstitch around the Brim ⅛ in/3 mm from the seam, making sure to catch the seam allowance in the topstitching.

STEP 5: FINISHING

A With **wrong** sides together, place the hat Lining inside the hat Exterior, making sure that the Crown center back seams and the Brim seams are lined up perfectly from the Exterior to the Lining. Pin all layers together. With the Exterior of the hat facing out, very carefully stitch in the ditch *(see page 26)* all hat layers together at the center back Crown seam and at both Brim seams. Please note that you will not want to catch the inside Casing in any of the stitching in the ditch. Baste all layers of the Brim outer edge together ⅜ in/1 cm from the edge.

B Using the double-fold binding made in step 2B, and starting at the back of the Brim, with **wrong** side of the hat and the Binding facing up, unfold the Binding and align the raw edge of Binding along the raw edge of the Brim. As you start, fold the short end of the Binding over ½ in/12 mm, **wrong** sides together, and pin in place. Continue pinning the Binding around the entire Brim. Once you reach the folded end of the Binding, overlap the Binding about ¾ in/2 cm. Sew the Binding to the Brim ⅝ in/16 mm from the edge. Wrap the Binding around the edge of the Brim, to the **right** side of the Brim, enclosing the raw edges. Fold the raw edge of the Binding under, along the crease, and edge stitch the Binding to the **right** side of the Brim.

C Pin a safety pin to one end of the shoelace and feed through the Casing. Draw the shoelace through the Casing and even out the ends, then loosely tie into a bow. Try your hat on, and adjust the shoelace until you get the fit you want.

Party

No
11

VINTAGE
BANNER

Nº 12

POM-POM PARTY POUF AND GARLAND

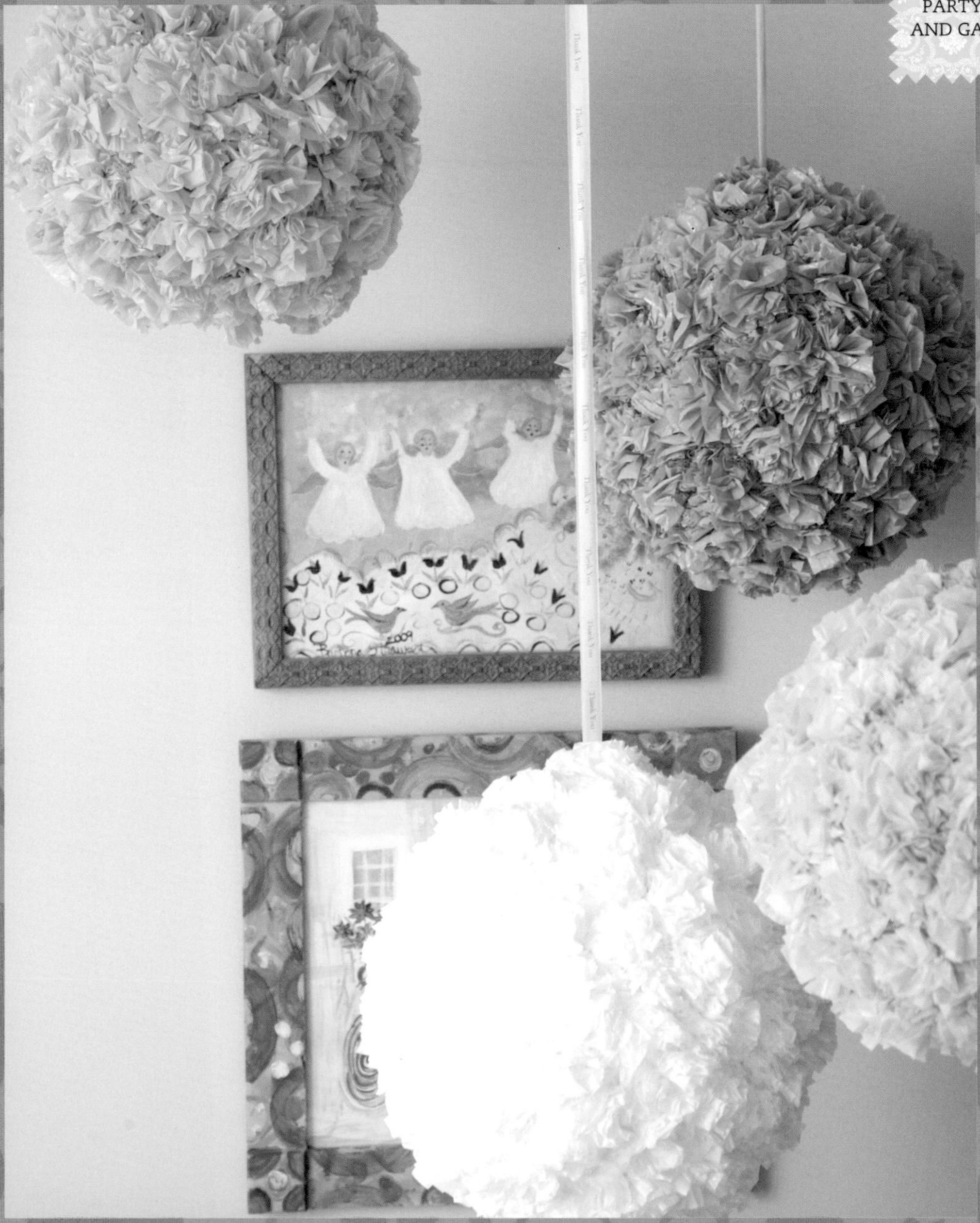

Nº
14
PRETTIEST
APRON

Vintage Banner

These banners are a perfect way to showcase small pieces of vintage ribbons, trims, or wallpaper that you may have on hand. You can create banners for inspiration, like the "Wish" banner pictured, or for any celebration. The banner would make a great gift for the parents of a new baby: spell the baby's name and coordinate the colors with those of the nursery. The banner adds a bit of cheerfulness wherever it is displayed.

NOTE: If you don't have enough of a beloved scrap of paper, take it to a local copy shop and have it copied in color onto card stock.

Finished size:

32 BY 14 IN/81 BY 35.5 CM

MATERIALS

- 15-by-9-in/38-by-23-cm rectangles of vintage wallpaper, scrapbook paper, or wrapping paper
- One 22-by-28-in/56-by-71-cm poster board sheet in a coordinating color for every 4 pennants
- One 25-ft/7.6-m roll tissue festooning
- One 3-in/7.5-cm scalloped white chipboard circle per letter (see Resources)
- One 2-in/5-mm chipboard alphabet set (see Resources)
- One 27-yd/24.7-m roll crepe paper streamer (1¾ in/4.5 cm wide)
- Two 16-in-/40.5-cm-long pieces of trim for each pennant (any combination of various vintage and new ribbons, fringe, and pom-pom fringe)
- 2 yd/2 m to 5 yd/4.5 m ribbon (½ in/12 mm to 1 in/2.5 cm wide) for hanging banner
- Fine glitter
- Small sponge brush

FROM THE CRAFT CABINET

- Tracing paper (optional)
- Pencil
- Scissors for paper
- White glue
- Newspaper to protect your work surface
- Paper plates
- Hot glue gun and glue sticks

CUTTING

Cut out (or trace with the tracing paper and the pencil) the pennant pattern piece provided in the front pocket of this book.

FROM POSTER BOARD:

Cut 1 pennant for each letter.
From the scraps of the poster board, cut out small 1-in/2.5-cm circles. They don't have to be perfect, since they are going on the back of the banner. You will need the same number of circles as pennant pieces, plus 1. For example, for the "Wish" banner we had 4 pennants and 5 circles on the back.

FROM DECORATIVE PAPER:

Cut 1 pennant for each letter.

ASSEMBLE

STEP 1: DECORATE PENNANTS

A   Place the chipboard letters on paper plates, **right** sides up. Using the small sponge brush, apply white glue to the **right** sides of the letters. Sprinkle glitter over the letters, making sure that the chipboard is entirely covered. Let the letters dry completely.

B   For each tassel, wrap the crepe streamer around your hand about 10 times, then slip off, keeping all the layers stacked on top of each other. Press the stack flat; there is now a crease at the top and bottom. You will have an approximately 5-by-1¾-in/12-by-4.5-cm rectangle with 20 layers of crepe paper. Fold the 2 corners at the top down to create a point, and secure the corners with glue. When the glue dries, starting at the bottom, make cuts through all the layers, spacing them about ¼ in/6 mm apart and stopping at the folded glued-down corners. Then cut off the bottom fold to create fringe. Make 1 tassel for each pennant. *(See illustration.)*

C   Glue the **wrong** side of the decorative paper pennant piece to a poster board pennant piece. Repeat for each pennant. Let the pennants dry completely.

D   Lay out the scalloped chipboard circles with the white sides up. With the hot glue gun, adhere each letter to the center of a circle. Let the glue dry completely.

E   Arrange the pennants in any order you find appealing, then place the scalloped circles with letters on each corresponding pennant to spell out the word or words you choose. The scalloped circles should be centered on each pennant about 3½ in/9 cm from the top edge. With the hot glue gun, glue the circles in place and let dry completely.

F   Attach the ribbons, trims, and fringes to each of the long straight edges of the pennants, using the hot glue gun. Let dry completely.

G   Attach 1 crepe paper tassel to each pennant point. Make sure to glue the side with the top folds to the **right** side of the pennant.

STEP 2: JOIN PENNANTS

A   Flip all the pennants over so the **wrong** sides are up. Your letters will now be backward. It is very important to make sure that your word(s) are spelled correctly and that the letters are in the proper order before continuing.

B   With the top corners of each pennant slightly overlapping, measure the width of the banner at the top and add 6 in/15 cm to that measurement. Cut a piece of ribbon to the longer measurement. Lay the ribbon across the backs of all the pennants, about ½ in/12 mm from the top edge, leaving 3-in/7.5-cm excess length at each end. With the hot glue gun, glue the ribbon in place. Make a small loop with the excess ribbon at each end. Glue the end of the ribbon to the back of the pennant. These loops will be what you hang the banner from. *(See illustration.)*

C   Glue the 1-in/2.5-cm poster board circles on top of the ribbon, where the tops of the pennants touch and at each end loop. These will add a bit of stability. Let the glue dry completely. *(See illustration.)*

D   Turn the entire banner **right**-side up. With the hot glue gun, glue the tissue paper festooning along the top of the banner.

E   Cut the extra ribbon in half, and tie each half into a pretty bow. Attach the bows at each end of the banner to help camouflage the hanging loops.

---

* STEP 1B *

Wrap crepe paper piece around hand and press flat, making 20 layers of crepe paper

Fold top corners down to create point and secure with glue

Starting at bottom folded edge make cuts through all layers, about ¼ in/6 mm apart

5 in/
12 cm

1¾ in/4.5 cm

Glue

Clip off bottom fold
to create fringe of tassel

* STEPS 2B & 2C *

Glue ribbon about ½ in/12mm
from top edge of pennants

Glue poster board circles
on top of ribbon where
pennants overlap and at
each end loop

Create loop with
excess ribbon

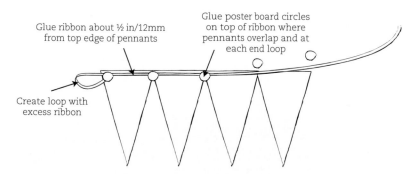

Wrong side of pennants face up,
and the top corners of each
pennant are slightly overlapped

Pom-Pom Party Pouf
and Garland

Jazz up your next celebration with this very easy and
oh-so-festive project. There is so much you can do with these
poufs and garlands: Make a whole bunch in different sizes
and colors to group together for a vibrant effect or create
a few in a single color for a more sophisticated look.

NOTE: The Party Poufs pictured have a diameter of about 12 in/30.5 cm;
we used an 8-in-/20-cm-diameter paper lantern as our base.
The garlands are each about 7 yd/6.5 m long.

Finished size:

VARIES, DEPENDING ON THE SIZE
OF PAPER LANTERN YOU USE AND HOW LONG
YOU WANT TO MAKE YOUR GARLAND

MATERIALS

- One 8-in/20-cm-diameter paper lantern
- 100 to 125 plastic pom-poms such as Just Fluff
- 10 to 12 yd/9 to 11 m Hug Snug seam binding (½ in/12 mm wide)

FROM THE CRAFT CABINET

- Hot glue gun and glue sticks

ASSEMBLE

STEP 1: LANTERN

A   Wrap the excess twist tie ends around the centers of the flat pom-poms, to get the ties out of the way. Do not remove the twist ties, because they hold the pom-poms together! Gently rub the layers of the pom-poms to separate and fluff out. This is a great step to do with kids or while you are watching a movie.

B   Carefully expand the paper lantern with the wire expander, following the manufacturer's instructions.

C   Starting at the top opening of the lantern, use the glue gun to glue the pom-poms in place. Hold each pom-pom for a few seconds to make sure that the glue sets, but be careful not to press too hard, as the paper lantern is delicate. The key is to place the pom-poms very close together and work your way around the entire top opening. Continue to glue the pom-poms around the lantern, working from top to bottom, until the entire lantern is completely covered. At the bottom opening of the lantern, you can use glue or a twist tie to attach 1 pom-pom to the center of the wire expander.

D   Cut a length of the seam binding for hanging the Party Pouf. Figure out where you want to hang it and measure the distance between the ceiling and the top of your Party Pouf. Multiply that number by 2. For example if you want the Party Pouf to hang 18 in/46 cm from the ceiling, you will want to cut a 36-in-/91-cm-long piece of seam binding. Fold the seam binding in half, slip the folded end through the top of the wire expander, then loop the loose ends of the seam binding through the folded end and pull tight. Knot the loose ends together. Glue 1 more pom-pom to the top of the wire expander, to close the top opening.

E   Let the glue dry completely.

STEP 2: GARLAND

A   Glue pom-poms to the remaining seam binding, spacing them 6 to 12 in/15 to 30.5 cm apart. Let the glue dry completely.

Posh Party Tablecloth and Napkins

Here are the ideal accessories for your next party. Who could say no to a ruffled tablecloth and napkins? The best part is that the tablecloth is reversible, so it's like getting two fancy tablecloths in one. The ruffled napkins with trim tie it all together.

Finished size of tablecloth (including ruffle):

VARIES, DEPENDING ON SIZE OF TABLE.
THE TABLECLOTH PICTURED MEASURES 102 BY 54 IN/
259 BY 137 CM AND HAS A 9-IN/23-CM RUFFLE.

Finished size of napkin (including ruffle):

22-IN/56-CM SQUARE

NOTE: The yardage requirements are for the tablecloth pictured, made to fit a 84-by-36 in/ 213-by-91-cm tabletop. To figure out the yardage you will need, grab a piece of paper, a pencil, a calculator, and a tape measure:

1   Measure the width of your tabletop and add 1 in/2.5 cm for the seam allowance.
2   Measure the length of your tabletop and add 1 in/2.5 cm for the seam allowance.
3   Divide the number from 2 by 36 in/100 cm to get the yardage/meters for the tabletop piece.
4   Add the width and length to get one-fourth of the ruffle length needed. Divide this number by 36 in/100 cm.
5   Add the figures from 3 and 4 to get the total yardage.
6   Add about ¼ yd/23 cm to ½ yd/45 cm for fabric shrinkage.

HERE IS AN EXAMPLE:

1   37 in/94 cm
2   85 in/216 cm
3   85 in/216 cm divided by 36 in/100 cm equals 2⅖ yd/2.2 m
4   37 in/94 cm plus 85 in/216 cm equals 122 in/310 cm, which divided by 36 in/100 cm equals 3⅖ yd/3.1 m
5   2⅖ yd/2.2 m plus 3⅖ yd/3.1 m equals 5⅘ yd/5.3 m
6   Total yardage for each side of the tablecloth = 6¼ yd/5.75 m

MATERIALS

FOR TABLECLOTH:

- 6¼ yd/5.75 m printed mid-weight cotton fabric (45 in/114 cm wide) for one side (Fabric A)
- 6¼ yd/5.75 m coordinating printed or solid mid-weight cotton fabric (45 in/114 cm wide) for second side (Fabric B)
- Coordinating thread

FOR NAPKINS:

Yardage given will yield 2 napkins.
- ⅝ yd/57 cm solid mid-weight cotton fabric (45 in/114 cm wide) for Napkin
- ⅝ yd/57 cm printed mid-weight cotton fabric (45 in/114 cm wide) for Ruffle (same as Tablecloth Fabric A)
- ⅜ yd/34 cm coordinating printed mid-weight cotton fabric (45 in/114 cm wide) for Trim (same as Tablecloth Fabric B)

FROM THE SEWING BASKET

- Water-soluble fabric marker
- Ruler
- Pins

- Scissors for fabric
- Small-gauge string or crochet cotton
- Hand sewing needle

CUTTING

FOR TABLECLOTH PIECES FROM FABRICS A AND B:

Lay both fabrics out flat, one on top of the other, **right** sides together. Using the fabric marker and the ruler, draw your tabletop dimensions onto the **wrong** side of the fabric. Pin the fabrics together and cut out.

FOR RUFFLE PIECES FROM FABRIC A:

Fold the remaining fabric in half, **right** sides together, and align the cut edges. Using the fabric marker and the ruler, draw four 10-in-/25-cm-wide strips, from the fold to the cut edges, onto the **wrong** side of the fabric. Pin the layers together and cut out.

FOR RUFFLE PIECES FROM FABRIC B:

Fold the remaining fabric in half, **right** sides together, and align the cut edges. Using the fabric marker and the ruler, draw four 10-in-/25-cm-wide strips, from the fold to the cut edges, onto the **wrong** side of the fabric. Pin the layers together and cut out. *(See fabric layout diagram.)*

NAPKINS

Fold all fabrics in half, **right** sides together, and align the selvage edges. Using the fabric marker and the ruler, draw the dimensions below onto the **wrong** side of the fabrics.

FROM NAPKIN FABRIC:

Cut two 19-in/48-cm squares.

FROM RUFFLE FABRIC:

Cut six 3-by-20-in/7.5-by-51-cm rectangles, on the fold.

FROM TRIM FABRIC:

Cut four 2-by-20-in/5-by-51-cm rectangles, on the fold. *(See fabric layout diagram.)*

ASSEMBLE

STEP 1: TABLECLOTH RUFFLE

A   Place 2 Ruffle pieces from fabric A, **right** sides together, and align them along 1 of the short ends, then pin. Sew together with a ½-in/12-mm seam allowance. Repeat until all 4 Ruffle pieces are joined into 1 long strip. Align the short ends of the long Ruffle, **right** sides together, and pin. Sew together with a ½-in/12-mm seam allowance. The Ruffle is now a big loop. Press the seams open.

B   Follow step 1A to join the fabric B Ruffle pieces.

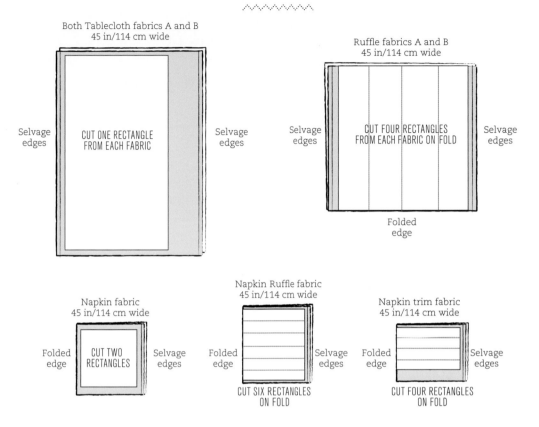

FABRIC LAYOUT DIAGRAM

Both Tablecloth fabrics A and B
45 in/114 cm wide

Selvage edges | CUT ONE RECTANGLE FROM EACH FABRIC | Selvage edges

Ruffle fabrics A and B
45 in/114 cm wide

Selvage edges | CUT FOUR RECTANGLES FROM EACH FABRIC ON FOLD | Selvage edges

Folded edge

Napkin fabric
45 in/114 cm wide

Folded edge | CUT TWO RECTANGLES | Selvage edges

Napkin Ruffle fabric
45 in/114 cm wide

Folded edge | | Selvage edges

CUT SIX RECTANGLES ON FOLD

Napkin trim fabric
45 in/114 cm wide

Folded edge | | Selvage edges

CUT FOUR RECTANGLES ON FOLD

C   Place the fabric A Ruffle loop inside the fabric B Ruffle loop with **right** sides together. Align the raw edges and match up the seams. Pin together along 1 of the long raw edges and sew together with a ½-in/12-mm seam allowance. Press the seam open, then fold **right**-side out so the Ruffle loops are **wrong** sides together. Align the raw edges. Press flat along the seam, which is now the bottom edge of the Ruffle.

D   Follow the instructions for gathering method two on page 23 along the raw edges of the Ruffle. Pull the string on the Ruffle and gather it to the approximate size of the outer perimeter of the Tablecloth piece.

E   With the fabric A Tablecloth piece right-side up on a flat surface, pin the Ruffle to the Tablecloth piece, making sure that the fabric A side of the Ruffle is against the **right** side of the fabric A Tablecloth piece. Align the raw edges and continue to pin around the perimeter, distributing the Ruffle gathers evenly. Once you are happy with the Ruffle gathers, sew the Ruffle to all 4 sides of the Tablecloth piece, ½ in/12 mm from the raw edges, pivoting at each corner. Clip the gathering string in a few places and pull out to remove.

STEP 2: TABLECLOTH FINISHING

A   Place the fabric A Tablecloth piece **right**-side up on a flat surface. Then place the fabric B Tablecloth piece on top of the fabric A piece, **right** sides together. Align all the raw edges and pin together. The Ruffle is now sandwiched between both Tablecloth pieces. Sew around the perimeter of the Tablecloth pieces with a ½-in/12-mm seam allowance. Pivot around each corner as you go. You will want to leave about a 12-in/30.5-cm opening along 1 edge, so the Tablecloth can be turned **right**-side out. Clip all the corners, and turn the Tablecloth **right**-side out.

B   Press the seam flat around the perimeter of the Tablecloth and Ruffle. On the fabric B Tablecloth, press the seam allowance under ½ in/12 mm at the opening. Then, with the hand sewing needle and thread, slipstitch the opening closed.

STEP 3: NAPKIN RUFFLE AND TRIM

A   Follow the French seam instructions on page 22 to join the short ends of 3 Ruffle pieces to make a loop. Press the seams to one side. Repeat with the other 3 Ruffle pieces.

B   Follow the baby hem instructions on page 18 to hem 1 of the long raw edges of each Ruffle piece.

C   Place 2 Trim pieces, **right** sides together, then align them along 1 of the short ends and pin. Sew together with a ¼-in/6-mm seam allowance. Repeat until all 4 Trim pieces are joined into 1 long strip. Press all the seams open. Fold 1 of the long raw edges over ½ in/12 mm, **wrong** sides together, and press.

STEP 4: NAPKIN FINISHING

A   Follow the instructions for gathering method two on page 23 along the raw edge of a Ruffle. Pull the string on the Ruffle and gather to the approximate size of the outer perimeter of a Napkin piece.

B   With the Napkin piece **wrong**-side up on a flat surface, pin the Ruffle to the Napkin, **wrong** sides together. Align the raw edges and continue to pin around the perimeter, distributing the Ruffle gathers evenly. Once you are happy with the gathers, baste the Ruffle to all 4 sides of the Napkin, ⅜ in/1 cm from the raw edges, pivoting at each corner. Clip the gathering string in a few places and pull out to remove. Lightly press so the Ruffle lies flat.

C   Starting at 1 corner of the Napkin, place the Trim piece on top of the basted Ruffle, **right** sides together. Align the raw edges and pin the Trim piece around the perimeter of the Napkin. You will need to clip into the seam allowance of the Trim piece at each corner. At the starting corner, begin sewing ½ in/12 mm from the corner and sew the Trim to the Napkin with a ½-in/12-mm seam allowance. Pivot around each corner as you go. When you reach the starting corner, fold back the trim sewn in the beginning so it doesn't get caught in the stitching, and end the sewing at the same spot where you started. Cut off the excess trim and save for the second napkin. *(See illustration.)*

D   With the Napkin and the Trim **wrong**-side up, fold and pinch out the excess Trim fabric at the corners; this will create neat mitered corners on the finished napkin. You want to make sure that the pressed edge of the Trim lies as flat as possible against the Ruffle and Napkin. The excess fabric at the corners, when pinched, creates a triangle. Fold this triangle over so it is flat. With the fabric marker, draw a straight line at a 45-degree angle, from the inside folded edge of the Trim to the stitching at the corner. Pinch the triangle and pin the excess together. Clip off the seam allowance at the corner, being careful not to cut the seam. Pull the Trim away from the Napkin and fold it flat against itself, with **right** sides together. Then sew the excess Trim together along the line drawn. Clip off the excess ¼ in/6 mm from the seam. *(See illustration.)*

E Turn the Trim over to the **right** side of the Napkin and press along the Ruffle/Trim seam. Pin the Trim to the Napkin and edge stitch in place, pivoting around the corners.

F Repeat steps 4A through 4E to make the second napkin.

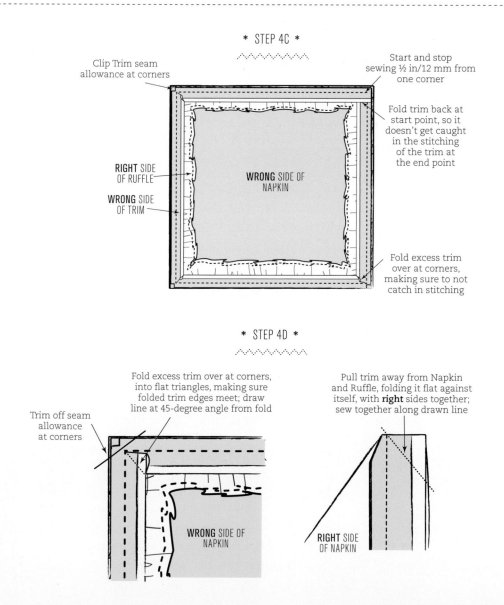

* STEP 4C *

Clip Trim seam allowance at corners

Start and stop sewing ½ in/12 mm from one corner

Fold trim back at start point, so it doesn't get caught in the stitching of the trim at the end point

RIGHT SIDE OF RUFFLE

WRONG SIDE OF TRIM

WRONG SIDE OF NAPKIN

Fold excess trim over at corners, making sure to not catch in stitching

* STEP 4D *

Fold excess trim over at corners, into flat triangles, making sure folded trim edges meet; draw line at 45-degree angle from fold

Pull trim away from Napkin and Ruffle, folding it flat against itself, with **right** sides together; sew together along drawn line

Trim off seam allowance at corners

WRONG SIDE OF NAPKIN

RIGHT SIDE OF NAPKIN

Prettiest Apron

Feminine styling with gathers and a high-waisted tie combine effortlessly in this useful apron. You could sew matching aprons for you and your daughter, or let both of your personalities shine with different fabric choices. This apron would make a lovely gift for that special hostess with the mostest in your life.

Finished sizes (not including ties):

SIZE	GIRLS' XS AND S	GIRLS' M AND L	WOMEN'S XS, S, AND M	WOMEN'S L AND XL
To fit bust measurements:	22 to 27 in/ 56 to 68.5 cm	27 to 32 in/ 68.5 to 81 cm	32 to 38 in/ 81 to 96.5 cm	38 to 44 in/ 96.5 to 112 cm
Length:	21 in/ 53 cm	25 in/ 63.5 cm	29 in/ 73.5 cm	33 in/ 84 cm

MATERIALS

PRINTED MID-WEIGHT COTTON FABRIC (45 IN/114 CM WIDE):

SIZE	GIRLS' XS AND S	GIRLS' M AND L	WOMEN'S XS, S, AND M	WOMEN'S L AND XL
Apron Fabric:	⅝ yd/ 57 cm	⅞ yd/ 80 cm	1 yd/ 1 m	1 yd/ 1 m
Tie/Binding Fabric:	⅜ yd/ 34 cm	⅜ yd/ 34 cm	⅜ yd/ 34 cm	⅜ yd/ 34 cm

FROM THE SEWING BASKET

- Water-soluble fabric marker or chalk pencil
- Ruler
- Scissors for fabric
- Pins
- Seam ripper
- Safety pin

CUTTING

FROM APRON FABRIC FOR THE APRON AND POCKET:

Place the fabric in a single layer with the **wrong**-side up. Using the fabric marker and the ruler, draw the dimensions below onto the **wrong** side of the fabric.

SIZE	GIRLS' XS AND S	GIRLS' M AND L	WOMEN'S XS, S, AND M	WOMEN'S L AND XL
Cut 1 rectangle (L by W):	22½ by 24 in/ 57 by 61 cm	26½ by 27 in/ 67 by 68.5 cm	29½ by 31 in/ 75 by 79 cm	33½ by 34 in/ 85 by 86 cm
Cut 1 rectangle (L by W):	6 by 6½ in/ 15 by 16.5 cm	6 by 6½ in/ 15 by 16.5 cm	8 by 8½ in/ 20 by 21.5 cm	8 by 8½ in/ 20 by 21.5 cm

After cutting out the Apron piece, you will want to draw a line, on the **wrong** side of the fabric, for the Casing placement. This line should be drawn straight across the width of the fabric, placed the distance below from one of the short ends.

SIZE	GIRLS' XS AND S	GIRLS' M AND L	WOMEN'S XS, S, AND M	WOMEN'S L AND XL
Casing placement from top edge of apron:	5½ in/ 14 cm	7 in/ 18 cm	8 in/ 20 cm	9 in/ 23 cm

FROM TIE/BINDING FABRIC:

Fold the fabric in half, **right** sides together, and align the selvage edges. Using the fabric marker and the ruler, draw the dimensions below on the **wrong** side of the fabric.
Cut six 1½-by-22-in/4-by-56-cm strips, *on the fold.* *(See fabric layout diagram.)*

* FABRIC LAYOUT DIAGRAM *

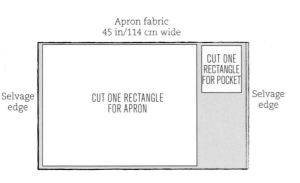

Apron fabric
45 in/114 cm wide

Selvage edge

CUT ONE RECTANGLE FOR APRON

CUT ONE RECTANGLE FOR POCKET

Selvage edge

Binding/Tie fabric
45 in/114 cm wide

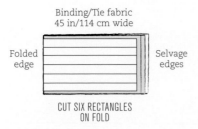

Folded edge

Selvage edges

CUT SIX RECTANGLES ON FOLD

ASSEMBLE

STEP 1: BINDING STRIPS, CASING, AND POCKET

A   Join 5 of the cross-grain Binding strips together, following the instructions on page 20. Then fold and press the joined strip into double-fold binding *(see page 20).*

B   Fold and press the remaining Binding strip into single-fold binding *(see page 19).* This will be the Casing for the Apron. Cut the Casing piece to the same width as the Apron.

C   Hem the short ends of the Casing by folding the raw edge over to the **wrong** side ¼ in/6 mm, and then press. Fold the edge over again, ¼ in/6 mm, and press. Edge stitch *(see page 21)* along the inner folded edge. Repeat on the other short end of the Casing. The Casing should now measure 1 in/ 2.5 cm less than the width of the Apron.

D   With **wrong** sides together, align the long top folded edge of the Casing along the drawn line of the Apron. Pin the Casing in place and make sure that the hemmed ends of the Casing are ½ in/ 12 mm from the raw edges of the Apron. Edge stitch the Casing in place along the top and bottom folded edges. *(See illustration.)*

E   With **wrong** sides facing up, unfold the Binding and align the raw edge of the Binding along 1 of the long raw edges of the Pocket. Pin in place. Sew the Binding to the Pocket ¼ in/6 mm from the edge. Wrap the Binding around the top of the Pocket to the **right** side of the Pocket, enclosing the raw edges. Fold the raw edge of the Binding under, along the crease, and edge stitch the Binding to the **right** side of the Pocket, making sure to cover the stitching that shows from the **wrong** side. Cut away any excess length of Binding from the raw edges.

F   With the Pocket **wrong**-side up, fold the 3 raw edges over ½ in/12 mm and press. With the Apron and the Pocket **right**-side up, place the Pocket on the Apron following the measurement below for the size you are making.

SIZE	GIRLS' XS, S, M, AND L	WOMEN'S XS, S, M, L, AND XL
Position down from Casing topstitch:	3 in/ 7.5 cm	6 in/ 15 cm
Position over from wearer's **right** raw edge:	2½ in/ 6 cm	3½ in/ 9 cm

G   Pin the Pocket in place. Edge stitch the Pocket to the Apron around the 3 folded edges, leaving the top bound edge open. If you like, you can reinforce each of the top corners by edge stitching and then backstitching ¼ in/6 mm parallel to the top edge.

STEP 2: FINISHING

A   Cut a piece of the double-fold Binding. The top edge of the Apron will be gathered into a specific measurement of the Binding. Cut the correct length of Binding for the size you are making, following the measurements below.

SIZE	GIRLS' XS AND S	GIRLS' M AND L	WOMEN'S XS, S, AND M	WOMEN'S L AND XL
Cut length of Binding:	7½ in/ 19 cm	8½ in/ 21.5 cm	10 in/ 25 cm	11 in/ 28 cm

B   Following gathering method one *(see page 23)*, place a row of basting stitches ¼ in/6 mm from the raw edge of the top of the Apron and another row ½ in/12 mm from the raw edge. Pulling the bobbin threads, gather the top edge to the same measurement as the length of the Binding cut in step 2A, making sure to distribute the gathers evenly.

C   With **wrong** sides facing up, unfold the Binding and align the raw edge along the top raw edge of the Apron. Pin in place. Sew the Binding to the Apron ¼ in/6 mm from the edge. Wrap the Binding around the top of the Apron to the **right** side of the Apron, enclosing the raw edges. Fold the raw edge of the Binding under, along the crease, and edge stitch the Binding to the **right** side of the Apron, making sure to cover the stitching that shows from the **wrong** side. *(See illustration.)* Remove any visible basting stitches with a seam ripper.

D   Cut 2 pieces of double-fold Binding that measure the length of the apron *plus* the neck tie length of 20 in/50 cm for girls' sizes and 23 in/58 cm for women's sizes. For example, if you are making the women's size XS, S, and M, you would cut 2 pieces of Binding that are 51 in/130 cm long.

E   Starting at the bottom edge of the Apron, with **wrong** sides together, unfold the double-fold Binding and align the raw edge along 1 of the side raw edges of the Apron. Pin in place. Sew the Binding to the Apron ¼ in/6 mm from the edge. Wrap the Binding around the side of the Apron to the **right** side of the Apron, enclosing the raw edges. Fold the raw edge of the Binding under, along the crease, and edge stitch the Binding to the **right** side of the Apron, making sure to cover the stitching that shows from the **wrong** side. Continue this edge stitch along the folded Binding edges that extend past the top edge of the Apron. This will enclose the raw edges of the Binding and create the neck Tie. Repeat on other side of the Apron. Tie a knot at each raw end of the Tie.

F   With the Apron **wrong**-side up, fold over the bottom edge of the Apron ¾ in/2 cm and press. Then fold over another ¾ in/2 cm and press again, pinning as needed. Edge stitch along the inner folded edge.

G   Edge stitch along the remaining folded Binding, enclosing the raw edges and making the waist Tie. Put a safety pin in a short end and use it to feed the Tie through the Casing so that even lengths of the Tie are visible at each end of the Casing. Tie a knot at each of the raw short ends of the waist Tie. Gather the Apron along the Casing to the desired width, and try it on.

* STEP 1D *

Place each hemmed
casing end ½ in/12 mm
from each side edge

Edge stitch
Casing in place

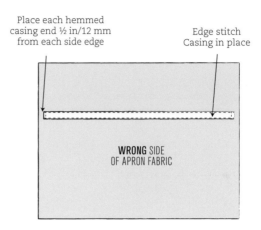

WRONG SIDE
OF APRON FABRIC

* STEP 2C *

With **wrong** side of
unfolded binding and fabric
facing up, align binding
along top edge and sew in
place with ¼-in/6-mm
seam allowance

Creases in
unfolded binding

Casing

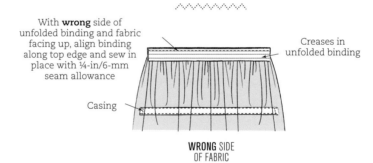

WRONG SIDE
OF FABRIC

Wrap binding over
top edge of Apron,
enclosing all raw
edges and edge
stitch in place

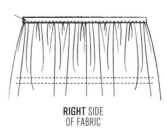

RIGHT SIDE
OF FABRIC

Sophia Stocking

Handmade Christmas stockings are wonderful. They can add
so much cheer to your holiday celebration, and they can be
used year after year. Here is a stocking that is festive even
when not overflowing with goodies. To get the lovely vintage
feel that ours has, search out some vintage matelassé
coverlets or quilts to use as fabric for the project.

Finished size:

23 IN/58 CM LONG AND 9 IN/23 CM WIDE AT OPENING

MATERIALS

- ¾ yd/70 cm matelassé or mid-weight home dec brocade fabric (54 in/137 cm wide) for Stocking and Cuff
- ¼ yd/23 cm coordinating mid-weight home dec fabric (54 in/137 cm wide) if making contrasting Cuff
- ⅝ yd/ 57 cm ribbon or trim for Cuff (optional)
- ¼ yd/23 cm ribbon (1 in/2.5 cm wide) for hanging loop
- Coordinating thread

FROM THE SEWING BASKET

- Tracing paper and pencil (optional)
- Water-soluble fabric marker
- Ruler
- Pins
- Scissors for fabric

CUTTING

Cut out (or trace with the tracing paper and the pencil) the Stocking pattern piece provided in the front pocket of this book.

FROM STOCKING AND CUFF FABRIC:

Fold the fabric in half, **right** sides together, and align the selvage edges.
Cut 2 Stocking pieces.
Using the water-soluble fabric marker and the   ruler, draw the dimensions below onto the **wrong** side of the fabric.
Cut two 6½-by-9½-in/16.5-by-24-cm rectangles, on the fold.

FROM CUFF FABRIC (IF DOING THE CONTRASTING CUFF):

Fold the fabric in half, **right** sides together, and align the selvage edges. Using the fabric marker and the ruler, draw the dimensions below onto the **wrong** side of the fabric.
Cut two 6½-by-19-in/16.5-by-49.5-cm rectangles. (See fabric layout diagram.)

NOTE: If the fabric you are using is too thick to make a double-layer Cuff, cut out only 1 of the Cuff rectangles. You will need to finish the bottom long raw edge of the Cuff by hemming it or attaching trim. Skip steps 2A and 2B, then follow only the first part of step 2C, omitting the instructions after "press seam open and turn Cuff **right**-side out."

* FABRIC LAYOUT DIAGRAM *

OPTION ONE:

Stocking/Cuff fabric
54 in/137 cm wide

Folded edge

CUT TWO RECTANGLES ON FOLD

Selvage edges

OPTION TWO:

Stocking fabric
54 in/137 cm wide

Folded edge

Selvage edges

Cuff fabric
54 in/137 cm wide

Folded edge

CUT TWO RECTANGLES

Selvage edges

ASSEMBLE

STEP 1: STOCKING

A   Place the Stocking pieces **right** sides together and pin around the curved edges. Sew together with a ½-in/12-mm seam allowance, leaving the top edge open.

B   Zigzag the edges together very close to the seam, and trim off the excess seam allowance. You will want to end up with about ¼-in/6-mm seam allowance. Home dec fabrics tend to fray a lot, and because of this, we can't clip into the seam allowance. We will remedy this a bit by trimming off the width of the seam allowance.

C   Fold the 1-in/2.5-cm ribbon in half, aligning the 2 short ends. Center the 2 short ends of the ribbon at the top back of the Stocking seam, with the **right** side of the ribbon against the **wrong** side of the Stocking. Align all raw edges. Pin in place, then baste the ribbon to the Stocking ¼ in/6 mm from edge. This will be the hanging loop for your stocking.

D   Turn the Stocking **right**-side out and press flat.

* STEP 2C *

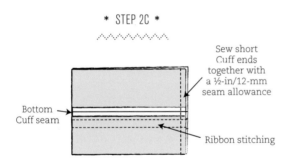

Sew short Cuff ends together with a ½-in/12-mm seam allowance

Bottom Cuff seam

Ribbon stitching

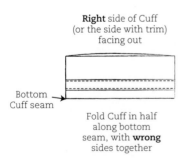

Right side of Cuff (or the side with trim) facing out

Bottom Cuff seam

Fold Cuff in half along bottom seam, with **wrong** sides together

STEP 2: CUFF AND FINISHING

A   Place Cuff pieces **right** sides together, and align all raw edges. Pin along 1 long edge and sew together with a ½-in/12-mm seam allowance. Unfold the piece and press the seam open.

B   If using the optional Cuff ribbon/trim, decide where you want to place it; it will only be sewn to 1 of the sewn-together Cuff pieces. The Cuff piece with the ribbon/trim will be referred to as the Cuff **right** side. Pin the ribbon/trim in place and topstitch it to the **right** side of the Cuff piece. If you would like to sew the ribbon/trim around the bottom edge, see step 2D.

C   Fold the Cuff piece in half widthwise, with **right** sides together, and align the raw edges of the 2 short ends. Pin in place. Sew the short ends together with a ½-in/12-mm seam allowance. Press the seam open and turn the Cuff **right**-side out; this is the back Cuff seam. Fold the Cuff in half along the bottom seam sewn in step 2A, with **wrong** sides together. Make sure to keep the side of the Cuff with ribbon/trim (if using) on the outside of the folded Cuff. Press flat, keeping the Cuff back seam along one of the folded edges. *(See illustration.)*

D   Follow this step only if you want to sew ribbon/trim along the bottom edge of the Cuff. Pin the ribbon/trim in place, then topstitch it to the bottom edge (the seamed edge) of the Cuff, making sure to fold under the short raw edge of the ribbon that will face out toward the **right** side. These instructions are a bit vague, because there are many different ways this can be done, depending on the type of ribbon/trim used. You can sew the ribbon/trim to the **right** side of the Cuff so the entire trim is visible, or you can sew the ribbon/trim to the **wrong** side of the Cuff if you only want a portion of the ribbon/trim to be visible. Play around with this to see what looks best.

E   Place the folded Cuff piece inside the Stocking with the Cuff **right** side against the Stocking **wrong** side. Align all the raw edges at the top opening, and match the back seam of the Cuff to the back seam of the Stocking, making sure that the hanging loop is sandwiched between the Stocking and the Cuff. Pin around the top edge. Sew around the top edge with a ½-in/12-mm seam allowance, then zigzag or serge the raw edge to finish. *(See illustration.)*

F   Pull the Cuff out of the Stocking and fold over the top opening. Press, and you are ready to hang your stocking.

* STEP 2E *

Place folded Cuff inside Stocking, with **right** side of Cuff against **wrong** side of Stocking

Make sure to match Cuff back seam with Stocking back seam

Ribbon hanging loop inside Stocking

Sew Cuff to Stocking together with a ½-in/ 12-mm seam allowance, around top opening

Dream

№
16
CROCHETED PILLOWCASE

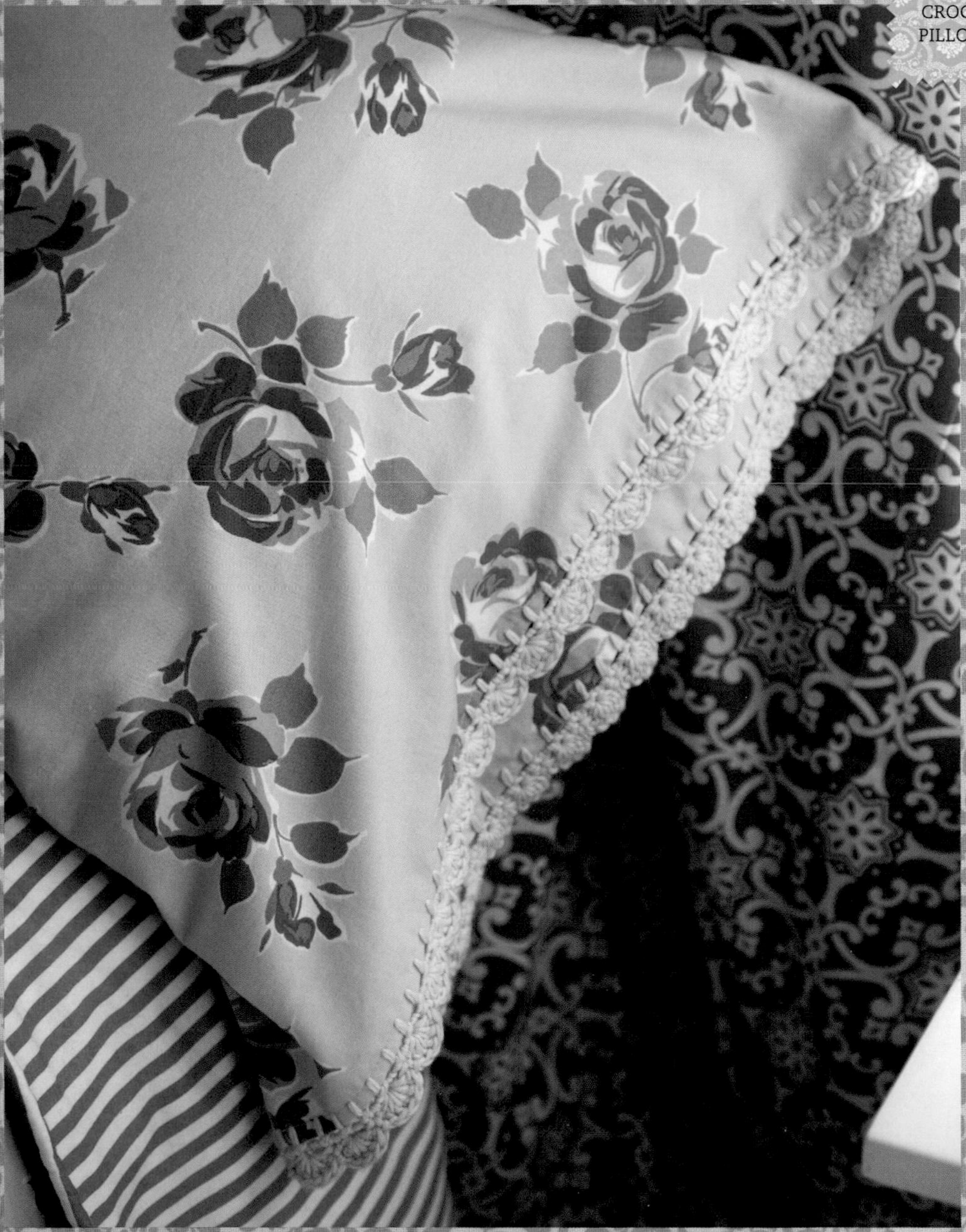

NO
16

Crocheted Pillowcase

CONTRIBUTED BY *Beata Basik*

Why settle for store-bought pillowcases? After making a couple of these, you'll be hooked (pardon the pun). You can do so much with fabric and color choice. For a girly gift, choose a floral fabric and finish it off with pink crochet trim. For the girl with more dramatic tastes, make a black and white striped pillowcase with red crochet trim. Don't stop with the pillowcases—you could easily add this trim to towels, down the front of a sweater, or along the hem of a skirt.

NOTE: If you are new to crochet or need to brush up on your skills you can watch some great how-to videos at www.nexstitch.com/tutorials.html.

Finished size (including crochet edging):

20 BY 29 IN/51 BY 75 CM

Gauge of crochet trim: 4 scallops = 4 in/10 cm

Crochet abbreviations:

ch = chain
slip st = slip stitch
sc = single crochet

dc = double crochet
* = the start of the
pattern repeat

MATERIALS

- 1¼ yd/1.2 m printed mid-weight cotton fabric (45 in/114 cm wide)
- 70 yd/64 m sport-weight cotton yarn such as Rowan Cotton Glace or Patons Grace
- Crochet hook U.S. size G/6/4 mm or size to obtain gauge
- Large chenille hand sewing needle
- Tapestry needle
- Coordinating thread

FROM THE SEWING BASKET

- Scissors for fabric
- Pins
- Water-soluble fabric marker or chalk pencil
- Ruler

CUTTING

With the fabric in a single layer, use the fabric marker and the ruler to draw the dimensions below onto the **wrong** side of the fabric.

FROM THE FABRIC:

Cut one 21-by-36-in/53-by-91-cm rectangle for Back. Cut one 21-by-29-in/53-by-73.5-cm rectangle for Front.

NOTE: Two layout options are provided; use the one that suits the direction of the print on your fabric. (*See fabric layout diagram.*)

ASSEMBLE

STEP 1: FRONT AND BACK

A Fold and press 1 short raw edge of the Back over ¼ in/6 mm, **wrong** sides together. Fold and press the same edge over ³⁄₈ in/1 cm. Pin the hem in place. Repeat on the Front piece.

B Edge stitch along the inner folded edge of the Back piece only. Keep the Front hem pinned.

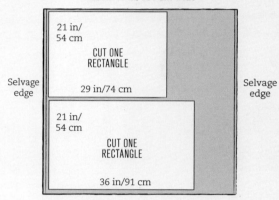

* FABRIC LAYOUT DIAGRAM *

OPTION 1:

Pillowcase Front and Back
fabric 45 in/114 cm wide

Selvage edge

21 in/54 cm

CUT ONE RECTANGLE

29 in/74 cm

21 in/54 cm

CUT ONE RECTANGLE

36 in/91 cm

Selvage edge

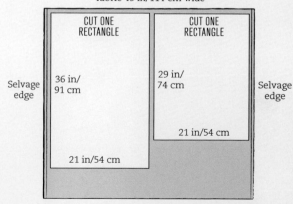

OPTION 2:

Pillowcase Front and Back
fabric 45 in/114 cm wide

Selvage edge

CUT ONE RECTANGLE

36 in/91 cm

21 in/54 cm

CUT ONE RECTANGLE

29 in/74 cm

21 in/54 cm

Selvage edge

C   Place the Back piece **right**-side up. Lay the Front on the Back with **right** sides together, and align along the 3 raw edges. The hemmed edge of the Back should extend 7 in/17 cm from the pinned edge of the Front. Fold the Back hemmed edge over the Front pinned edge (you may need to adjust the pins on the Front hem so they don't extend past the folded edge), creating an overlap. *(See illustration.)* Pin the pieces together along the 3 raw edges.

D   Sew the raw edges with a ½-in/12-mm seam allowance. Clip off the corners and then finish the raw edges in your preferred method. *(See illustration.)*

E   Flip the Back overlap onto the Back piece so the **wrong** sides are together, creating a pocket. Press the Back folded edge so it is even with the Front pinned edge. Adjust the stitch length on your sewing machine to 3; you will want there to be 9 or 10 stitches per 1 in/2.5 cm when sewing around the top edge of the pillowcase (the correct stitch length will help keep the blanket stitches evenly spaced). Starting at the Front, sew around the top edge of pillowcase, about ¼ in/6 mm from folded edge. This will finish the hem on the Front piece and add topstitching to the Back.

F   Turn the pillowcase **right**-side out and press flat.

STEP 2: BLANKET STITCH

A   Cut a 6-yd/5.5-m length of yarn. Thread the yarn through the chenille needle, pulling it through the needle and matching up the cut ends. Tie the ends into a knot.

B   To hide the knot, pull the threaded needle up between the Back of the pillowcase and the back pocket and out the top folded edge of the pillowcase. This can be a bit fussy because of the topstitching, but to make a nice clean start for the blanket stitching, it is best to have the yarn coming out of the top folded edge.

C   Blanket stitch *(see page 20)* around the entire top (open) edge of the pillowcase. To keep your stitches evenly spaced and the same width, use the topstitching around the top edge as a guide. Pull the needle up through the fabric, directly below every fourth stitch of the topstitching. Make sure not to pull the stitches too tight; if you do, the fabric between the stitches will collapse.

D   When you get close to where you started, count the remaining topstitches you are using as a guide. If you don't have a number divisible by 4, fudge the spacing a bit so it looks even, but try to end with an even number of blanket stitch loops. Once you reach the first stitch you made, pull the needle back down inside the pillowcase pocket and tie a knot to secure the stitches. Cut off the excess yarn.

STEP 3: CROCHET TRIM

ROUND 1   Starting where you began the blanket stitching, join the yarn to the top loop of the blanket stitch with a slip st (making sure to leave at least a 6-in/15-cm yarn tail to weave in later); ch 1, work 2 sc into same blanket stitch loop, then work 2 sc in each blanket stitch loop around, join with a slip st in first sc—the total number of sc's should be divisible by 4.

ROUND 2   *Skip 1 sc, work 5 dc in the next sc, skip 1 sc, slip st into next sc; rep from * around, end with a slip st in skipped sc at beginning of round. Cut yarn, leaving a 6-in/15-cm tail. Using the tapestry needle, weave tails into the crochet to secure.

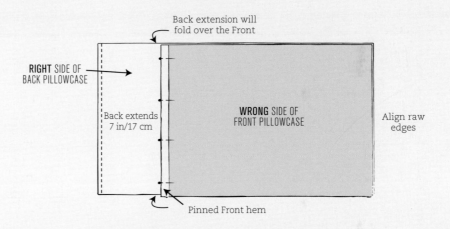

Back extension will fold over the Front

RIGHT SIDE OF BACK PILLOWCASE

Back extends 7 in/17 cm

WRONG SIDE OF FRONT PILLOWCASE

Align raw edges

Pinned Front hem

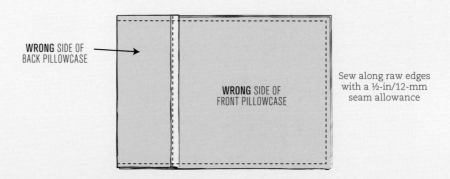

WRONG SIDE OF BACK PILLOWCASE

WRONG SIDE OF FRONT PILLOWCASE

Sew along raw edges with a ½-in/12-mm seam allowance

Box Pleat Bed Skirt

The box pleat construction is sophisticated, while the feminine fabric choice makes the skirt girly. It provides a neat and polished look, and now no one has to know what is under your bed. We left the corners open at the foot of the bed, to accommodate posts. If your bed has a footboard, omit the skirt from this section.

NOTE: These instructions are for a twin-size bed skirt, but can easily be used for any size bed. The instructions are the same. You'll just use different dimensions and more yardage. For the bed skirt pictured here, we cut the fabric along the length grain, to avoid having to seam the skirt pieces. Please keep that in mind when choosing prints.

Finished size:

TO FIT TWIN BOX SPRING WITH A 12-IN/30.5-CM SKIRT

MATERIALS

Note that your yardage will vary depending on the size of your bed and how long you want the skirt to be.

- 4¾ yd/4.3 m printed mid-weight cotton fabric (45 in/114 cm wide) for Skirt
- 4¾ yd/4.3 m muslin (45 in/114 cm wide) for Lining
- 1 twin-size fitted sheet that fits box spring
- Coordinating thread

FROM THE SEWING BASKET

- Water-soluble fabric marker
- Ruler
- Pins
- Scissors for fabric

* FABRIC LAYOUT DIAGRAM *

Use fabric layout for both
Bed Skirt and Lining fabrics
45 in/114 cm wide

Selvage edges

Selvage edges

CUT THREE RECTANGLES
FROM EACH FABRIC ON FOLD

Folded edge

CUTTING

To figure out the yardage you need, measure each side of the box spring you want to put the skirt on. Multiply each number by 2, then add 1 in/2.5 cm for seam allowance. A twin box spring measures 75 by 39 in/191 by 99 cm. We put a skirt on both of the long sides and at the foot. So the length of fabric we need for each would be 151 in/384 cm for the 2 long sides and 79 in/201 cm for the foot. Then measure from the top edge of the box spring to the floor to get the finished skirt length. For the cut skirt measurement, add 1½ in/4 cm to the finished measurement. Our finished skirt measurement was 12 in/30.5 cm, so the cut measurement would be 13½ in/34 cm. For the cut lining measurement, add ½ in/12 mm to the finished skirt measurement. Our lining cut measurement is 12½ in/32 cm.

To get the yardage/meter requirements, take the longest measurement (ours is 151 in/384 cm) and divide that by 36 in/100 cm (we got 4⅕ yd/3.8 m), then round that measurement up ½ to ¾ yd/45 to 70 cm, for shrinkage and a little wiggle room. So here are the cutting dimensions for our twin-size Skirt and Lining:

FROM SKIRT FABRIC:

Fold the fabric in half, **right** sides together, and align cut edges. Using the fabric marker and the ruler, draw the dimensions below onto the **wrong** side of the fabric.
Cut two 75½-by-13½-in/192-by-34-cm rectangles, on the fold.
Cut one 39½-by-13½-in/100-by-34-cm rectangle, on the fold.

FROM LINING FABRIC:

Fold the fabric in half, **right** sides together, and align cut edges. Using the fabric marker and the ruler, draw the dimensions below onto the **wrong** side of the fabric.

Cut two 75½-by-12½-in/192-by-32-cm rectangles, on the fold.
Cut one 39½-by-12½-in/100-by-32-cm rectangle, on the fold.
(See fabric layout diagram.)

ASSEMBLE

STEP 1: SKIRT AND LINING

A   With **right** sides together, align 1 Skirt piece and 1 Lining piece along 1 long end, and pin. Sew together with a ½-in/12-mm seam allowance and press the seam allowance toward the Skirt. Repeat on the remaining Skirt and Lining pieces.

B   Fold a joined Skirt and Lining piece in half lengthwise, with **right** sides together, and align along the long raw edge. Since the Lining piece is shorter than the Skirt piece, the Skirt fabric will roll ½ in/12 mm toward the Lining side. Align the short raw edges and pin. Sew together with a ½-in/12-mm seam allowance. Trim off the corners, turn **right**-side out, and press flat. Repeat this step on the other joined piece. *(See illustration.)*

C   With **wrong** sides together, run a basting stitch along the top raw edge, ½ in/12 mm from the edge. Repeat for each Skirt piece.

STEP 2: PLEATS

NOTE: When marking pleats on the Skirt side panels, the end where you start marking will be the foot of the bed. Make sure to start on opposite ends of the 2 panels, to achieve a mirror image of the pleat placement. If you need to adjust or fudge pleat placement or size, do so on the end closest to the head of the bed. When marking pleats on the foot panel, find the center of the panel and mark the pleats from the center out. You want the pleats to be placed evenly from the center. Therefore, make any necessary adjustments at the ends.

A   With a side Skirt piece **right**-side up, make a mark every 5 in/12 cm along the top raw edge using the fabric marker and the ruler. Repeat on the other Skirt piece.

B   With the fabric **right**-side up, fold the fabric with **wrong** sides together. Align the first and third marks, and pin together. Secure the pleat by sewing through all layers straight down from the aligned marks about 3 in/7.5 cm. Repeat with all the odd-numbered pleat markings, making sure to skip the even-numbered marks. *(See illustration.)*

C   When all pleats are made and secured, you will now flatten them to create a box pleat. With the fabric **right**-side up, find the mark at the center fold of the pleat. Align that mark with the seam created when you secured marks 1 and 3 together in step 2B. There should now be equal folds of fabric on each side of the pleat. With the top raw edges aligned, baste the pleat down ¼ in/6 mm from the edge. Repeat on all other pleats. *(See illustration.)*

STEP 3: FINISHING

A   Place the fitted sheet on the box spring. With the fabric marker and the ruler, draw straight lines on the sheet along the top edges of the box spring.

B While the fitted sheet is still on the box spring, with **right** sides together, pin the raw edge of the Skirt along the drawn line. When pinning the Skirt to the sheet, be careful not to pin through to the box spring. Repeat for each skirt piece to be attached. Remove the sheet from the box spring. With the **wrong** side of the Skirt facing up, sew the Skirt to the sheet, ½ in/12 mm from the raw edge, using the basting you did in step 1C as your guide. *(See illustration.)*

C Fold the Skirt over the seam allowance and press. With the Skirt **right**-side up, topstitch the Skirt to the sheet ¼ in/6 mm from the seam.

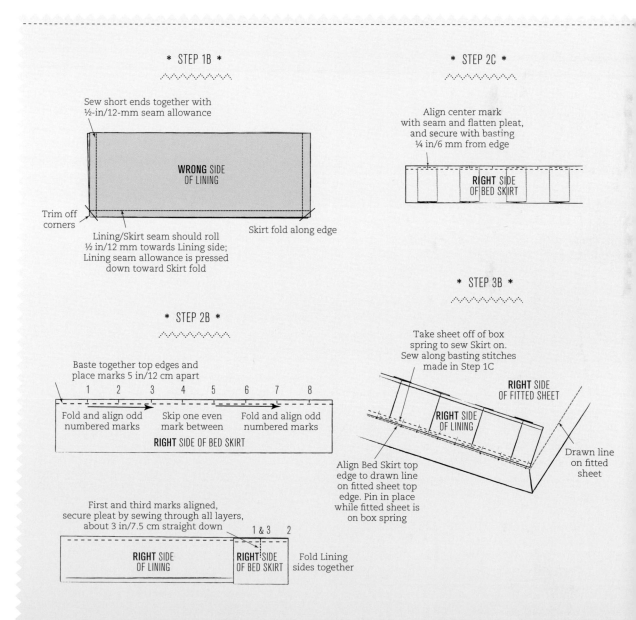

* STEP 1B *

Sew short ends together with ½-in/12-mm seam allowance

WRONG SIDE OF LINING

Trim off corners

Lining/Skirt seam should roll ½ in/12 mm towards Lining side; Lining seam allowance is pressed down toward Skirt fold

Skirt fold along edge

* STEP 2B *

Baste together top edges and place marks 5 in/12 cm apart

1   2   3   4   5   6   7   8

Fold and align odd numbered marks   Skip one even mark between   Fold and align odd numbered marks

RIGHT SIDE OF BED SKIRT

First and third marks aligned, secure pleat by sewing through all layers, about 3 in/7.5 cm straight down

1 & 3   2

RIGHT SIDE OF LINING

RIGHT SIDE OF BED SKIRT

Fold Lining sides together

* STEP 2C *

Align center mark with seam and flatten pleat, and secure with basting ¼ in/6 mm from edge

RIGHT SIDE OF BED SKIRT

* STEP 3B *

Take sheet off of box spring to sew Skirt on. Sew along basting stitches made in Step 1C

RIGHT SIDE OF FITTED SHEET

RIGHT SIDE OF LINING

Align Bed Skirt top edge to drawn line on fitted sheet top edge. Pin in place while fitted sheet is on box spring

Drawn line on fitted sheet

NO

18

Madeline Quilt

CONTRIBUTED BY *Nancy Geaney*

Here is a quilt that's easy enough for the beginner, yet still fun for the more experienced quilter. We pieced the quilt together with fabrics from the Sis Boom fabric line. Feel free to play around with color, layout, and fabric, to get the result you desire.

NOTE: There are many ways to finish your quilt. The quilt pictured was quilted with a long arm quilting machine. Most of us don't have one of those, but many companies can do the finishing work for you. See the Resources section for more information. If you want to do the quilting yourself, use your preferred method, whether free motion, stitching in the ditch, hand tying, or even hand quilting.

Finished size:

85½ BY 68½ IN/ 217 BY 174 CM

MATERIALS

- ⅝ yd/57 cm of 10 different mid-weight cotton fabrics (45 in/114 cm wide) for Top
- 5 yd/4.5 m mid-weight cotton fabric (45 in/114 cm wide) for Backing
- ⅝ yd/57 cm mid-weight cotton fabric (45 in/114 cm wide) for Binding
- Twin-bed-size cotton batting
- Light-colored neutral 100 percent cotton thread for piecing
- Coordinating 100 percent cotton thread for quilting
- Coordinating embroidery floss (for hand-tied only)

FROM THE SEWING BASKET

- Scissors for fabric
- Rotary cutter and cutting mat (optional, but it makes cutting all those pieces a lot easier)
- Pins
- Hand sewing needle
- Safety pins (optional)
- Clear gridded ruler
- Darning foot for your sewing machine (for free-motion quilting)
- Walking foot for your sewing machine (for stitch in the ditch or straight line quilting)

FROM THE CRAFT CABINET

- Masking tape
- Quilt basting spray (temporary fabric adhesive)

CUTTING

FROM EACH OF THE 10 TOP FABRICS:

Fold the fabric in half, **right** sides together, and align the selvage edges. Trim off the selvage edges. Keep the fabric folded in half. With the gridded ruler and the rotary cutter, square off the top edges. Measure 18 in/43 cm down from the top edge and cut across the width of fabric. Keep this piece folded in half and cut it into 2 pieces, one 6-in/15-cm piece and one 12-in/30-cm piece. Discard any scraps. You should have a long 6-in-/15-cm-wide piece and a long 12-in/30-cm piece.

Cut the 6-in/15-cm piece into:
- Three 6-by-12-in/15-by-30-cm rectangles
- One 6-in/15-cm square

Cut the 12-in/30-cm piece into:
- Two 12-in/30-cm squares
- Two 6-by-12-in/15-by-30-cm rectangles
- Two 6-in/15-cm squares

FROM BACKING FABRIC:

Fold the fabric in half, with **right** sides together, and align the cut edges. Using the fabric marker and
the ruler, draw the dimensions below onto the **wrong** side of the fabric.
Cut two 90-by-35.5-in/229-by-90-cm rectangles.

FROM BINDING FABRIC:

Fold the fabric in half, **right** sides together, and align the selvage edges. Using the fabric marker and
the ruler, draw the dimensions below onto the **wrong** side of the fabric.
Cut eight 2½-in/6-cm-wide cross grain strips, on the fold *(see page 20)*, so when pieced together they
measure 8¾ yd/8 m long. *(See fabric layout diagram.)*

* FABRIC LAYOUT DIAGRAM *

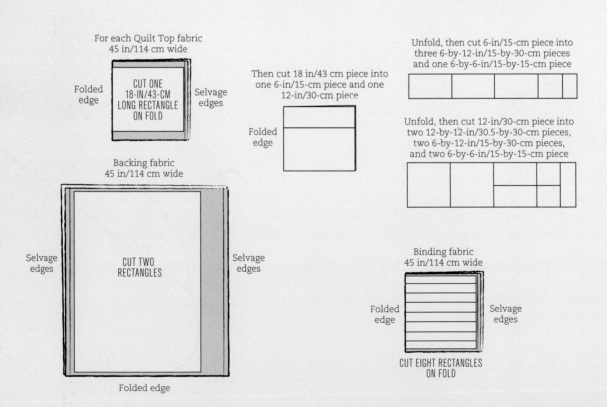

ASSEMBLE

STEP 1: QUILT BLOCKS

A   Randomly select one 6-in/15-cm square and one 6-by-12-in/15-by-30-cm piece. Align the 6-in/15-cm raw edges and pin. Sew together with a ¼-in/6-mm seam allowance. Press the seam allowance toward the rectangle. *(See illustration.)*

B   Randomly select one 12-in/30-cm square piece and one 6-by-12-in/15-by-30-cm piece. Align the 12-in/30-cm raw edges and pin. Sew together with a ¼-in/6-mm seam allowance. Press the seam allowance toward the rectangle. *(See illustration.)*

C   Align the 2 sewn pieces along the raw edges, **right** sides together, and pin. Make sure that the vertical seams are matched up. Sew together with a ¼-in/6-mm seam allowance. Press the seam allowance to one side. *(See illustration.)*

D   Repeat steps 1A to 1C until you have 20 complete blocks.

E   With the ruler and the rotary cutter, square up and trim each block to a 17½-in/44.5-cm square.

F   In a random manner, arrange the blocks in a 4-by-5 grid. Move and rotate them around until you're happy with the overall layout.

STEP 2: TOP

A   Starting with the top horizontal row, pin and sew all the blocks, **right** sides together, with a ¼-in/6-mm seam allowance. Press the seam allowances to the left. Return the completed strip to the layout.

B   Sew the second horizontal row of blocks, **right** sides together, with a ¼-in/6-mm seam allowance. Press all the seam allowances to the right. Return the strip to the layout.

C   Repeat steps 2A and 2B until you have 5 horizontal strips of 4 blocks each. Make sure that the strips have the seam allowances pressed in alternating directions (left, right, left, and so on). This will help reduce bulk and interlock the strips when they are sewn together.

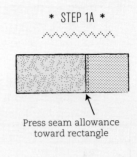

* STEP 1A *

Press seam allowance toward rectangle

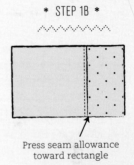

* STEP 1B *

Press seam allowance toward rectangle

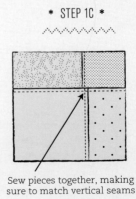

* STEP 1C *

Sew pieces together, making sure to match vertical seams

Darcy Duvet

Here's an instant pick-me-up for your bed and a quick weekend project to boot. Don't let the size of the project scare you— duvets are very simple to sew and provide dramatic results. This one uses a different fabric on each side, so it's a cinch to change the mood of your bedroom by just flipping the comforter over!

NOTE: These instructions are for a twin-size comforter, but can easily be used for any size comforter. The instructions are the same. The only things that need to be changed are the cut dimensions and in some cases the yardage. Measure the length and width of your comforter and add 2 in/5 cm to these measurements for seam allowance and ease. The yardage given may be enough to make a queen-size duvet.

NOTE: If you are using a large-scale print and want it to match at the seams, you will need to buy extra yardage. Please see page 17 for tips on how to figure this out.

Finished size to fit a twin-bed comforter:

90 BY 68 IN/229 BY 173 CM

MATERIALS

- 6 yd/5.5 m printed mid-weight cotton fabric (45 in/114 cm wide) for one side (Fabric A)
- 6 yd/5.5 m coordinating printed or solid mid-weight cotton fabric (45 in/114 cm wide) for second side (Fabric B)
- ¾ yd/70 cm coordinating mid-weight cotton fabric (45 in/114 cm wide) for bias Piping
- 9 yd/8.3 m cotton filler cord (³/₁₆ in/5 mm)
- One 60-in/152-cm coordinating zipper
- Coordinating thread

FROM THE SEWING BASKET

- Water-soluble fabric marker
- Ruler
- Pins
- Scissors for fabric
- Zipper foot for sewing machine
- Seam ripper

CUTTING

FROM FABRIC A:

Cut the fabric length in half so you have two 3-yd-/2.75-m-long pieces.

Fold 1 piece in half, with **right** sides together, and align the selvage edges. Using the fabric marker and the ruler, draw the dimensions below onto the **wrong** side of the fabric.

Cut one 91-by-21-in/231-by-53-cm rectangle, on the fold.

Fold the other piece in half, with **right** sides together, and align the selvage edges. Using the fabric marker and the ruler, draw the dimensions below onto the **wrong** side of the fabric.

Cut two 91-by-14½-in/231-by-37-cm rectangles.

FROM FABRIC B:

Repeat the Fabric A cutting instructions.

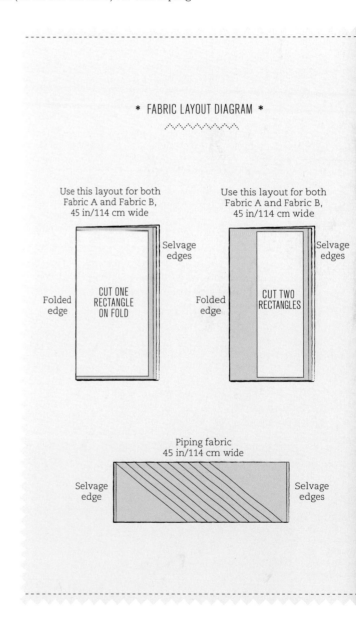

* FABRIC LAYOUT DIAGRAM *

Use this layout for both Fabric A and Fabric B, 45 in/114 cm wide

Selvage edges

Folded edge

CUT ONE RECTANGLE ON FOLD

Use this layout for both Fabric A and Fabric B, 45 in/114 cm wide

Selvage edges

Folded edge

CUT TWO RECTANGLES

Piping fabric 45 in/114 cm wide

Selvage edge

Selvage edges

FROM PIPING FABRIC:

With the fabric in a single layer:
Cut enough 1¾-in/4.5-cm-wide bias-grain binding strips *(see page 20)*, so when pieced together they measure 9 yd/8.3 m long. *(See fabric layout diagram.)*

ASSEMBLE

STEP 1: DUVET PIECES

A   Follow the French seam instructions on page 22 to join the long edge of the wide fabric A rectangle to the long edge of 1 narrow fabric A rectangle. Repeat on the other long edge of the wide fabric A rectangle with the second narrow fabric A rectangle. Press the seams toward the center.

B   Repeat step 1A with the fabric B rectangles, except press the seams toward the outside edges.

STEP 2: PIPING

A   Following the instructions on page 20, join all the bias strips into 1 long piece.

B   Put the zipper foot on the sewing machine, and keep the foot on until the last step. With the bias strip **wrong**-side up, place the filler cord down the center of the strip. Fold the bias strip in half lengthwise. Align the raw edges, encasing the filler cord, then pin. Sew the raw edges together as close to the encased filler cord as possible. You will end up with about a ½-in/12-mm seam allowance from the raw edge to the stitching. The total width of the Piping should be about ⅞ in/2.2 cm. *(See illustration.)*

C   With the fabric A duvet piece **right**-side up, align the Piping along 1 of the raw edges. Begin and end the Piping at a long side edge. Pin the Piping in place around the entire perimeter of the duvet piece, clipping into the Piping seam allowance at each corner. There will be some excess Piping at the end; leave it for now. Starting 1 in/2.5 cm from the beginning of the Piping, sew the Piping to the duvet piece with a ½-in/12-mm seam allowance, pivoting around each corner. Stop sewing about 2 in/5 cm from where the beginning of the Piping meets the end of the Piping. Overlap the Piping 1 in/2.5 cm and cut off the excess. With a seam ripper, take out 1 in/2.5 cm of the stitching on the end of the Piping fabric, to expose the cord. Lay the exposed cord along the duvet, line it up with the beginning of the Piping, and cut off the excess exposed cord so that the ends of the cord just meet. Fold under the "empty" end of the Piping fabric ½ in/12 mm and wrap around the beginning of the Piping. Pin in place. Finish sewing the remaining Piping in place. *(See illustration.)*

STEP 3: FINISHING

A   With the fabric A duvet piece **right**-side up, center the zipper along 1 short end, **right** side down, and align the zipper tape with the raw edge. Pin in place. Sew the zipper to the duvet with a ¼-in/6-mm seam allowance. Repeat on the fabric B duvet piece with the opposite edge of the zipper tape. Open the zipper. *(See illustration.)*

B Place both duvet pieces, **right** sides together, align all raw edges, and pin. Sew together with a
½-in/12-mm seam allowance, starting and stopping at each end of the zipper. Trim the corners.
Put the regular foot back on your sewing machine and finish the raw edges in your preferred
method. Turn the duvet **right**-side out through the zipper opening.

* STEP 2B *

Raw edges

RIGHT SIDE
OF FABRIC

Encased
filler cord

Sew together
close to filler cord

* STEP 3A *

RIGHT SIDE
OF DUVET

Center zipper on one of the short ends,
right sides together; sew zipper in place
with ¼-in/6-mm seam allowance

* STEP 2C *

RIGHT SIDE
OF DUVET

Overlap ends of
Piping 1 in/2.5 cm
cut off excess Piping

Stop sewing Piping to
Duvet, 2 in/5 cm from the
beginning end of Piping

Start sewing Piping
to Duvet, 1 in/2.5 cm
from end of Piping

RIGHT SIDE
OF DUVET

Wrap the empty end
of fabric around the
beginning end of Piping

Finish sewing
Piping in place

Raw edge
folded
under

Fold raw edge of Piping
fabric over ½ in/12 mm,
wrong sides together

Take out stitching
of Piping on longer
loose end to expose cord

Cut exposed cord so
the ends of cord meet

RIGHT SIDE
OF DUVET

Fancy Fabric-Covered Headboard

CONTRIBUTED BY *Mary Tucciarone and Maritza Bermudez*

A headboard may seem like an ambitious project, but this one is quite easy. Best of all, you can create any mood or look you desire by using different fabrics and shapes. Play around first, to determine which shape works best. A simple way to decide on the shape you want is by using masking tape to trace the desired shape and size on your wall.

NOTE: Since headboard sizes can vary, these instructions do not give actual amounts for supplies; make measurements based on the size of your headboard. We give you two options for the headboard base material: ½ in/12 mm plywood or ⅜-in/1-cm FirmaFlex. There are good reasons to use each. Plywood is affordable and widely available; FirmaFlex is easy to use and very lightweight. The headboard pictured has a FirmaFlex base.

Finished size of headboard pictured:

60 BY 40 IN/152 BY 102 CM

MATERIALS

- 1 piece of ½-in/12-mm plywood or ⅜-in/1-cm FirmaFlex, cut to headboard dimensions
- 1 sheet of 1-in/2.5-cm foam approximately same size as headboard
- 1 piece of cotton quilt batting at least 4 in/10 cm larger than headboard on all sides
- 1 seamed piece of printed or solid mid-weight cotton fabric at least 4 in/10 cm larger than headboard on all sides
- Staple gun and staples
- Utility knife
- Spray adhesive
- Flush mounts or French cleat for mounting headboard
- ½-in/12-mm flathead screws, to screw mounts to headboard
- Longer flathead screws, appropriate for your type of wall, to screw mount/s into wall
- Drop cloth or newspaper to cover work surface when using spray adhesive

NOTE: Since the fabric isn't wide enough for most headboards, you will need to create a piece of fabric large enough. See below for instructions. If you are using a large-scale print and want it to match at the seams, you will need to buy extra yardage. Please see page 17 for tips on how to figure this out.

FROM THE SEWING BASKET

- Scissors for fabric
- Pins
- Water-soluble fabric marker or chalk pencil
- 65-mm rotary cutter (if using FirmaFlex) and mat
- Ruler

FROM THE CRAFT CABINET

Power drill with drill and screw bits

CUTTING

PLYWOOD:

Have the hardware or lumber store cut the plywood to your headboard dimensions. If you desire rounded edges or curved shapes, these will have to be done with a jigsaw.

FIRMAFLEX:

You can do straight cuts yourself with a 65-mm rotary cutter, mat, and ruler. If you desire rounded edges or curved shapes, these will have to be done with a jigsaw. Refer to the manufacturer's instructions for cutting.

FOAM:

Lay the headboard base on top of the foam. Use the utility knife to cut the foam to the same size as the headboard base.

QUILT BATTING AND SEAMED FABRIC:

Using scissors, cut both so they measure at least 4 in/10 cm larger on all sides than the headboard base. *(See illustration.)*

ASSEMBLE

STEP 1: FABRIC PANELS

A   Cut off the selvage edges from the fabric, and measure the width of the fabric. This will be the center of the pieced fabric for your headboard. Determine the remaining width needed on each side of the headboard, and cut the fabric to that width. For example, if your headboard is 60 in/ 152 cm wide, you will need a finished piece of fabric that is at least 68 in/173 cm wide. The center panel of the fabric measures 42 in/107 cm, without selvages, so you will need two 13-in-/ 33-cm-wide panels for each side. Add 1 in/2.5 cm to the side panel width for seam allowances.

B   Align the raw edges of the middle panel to 1 side panel and pin. Sew together with a ½-in/ 12-mm seam allowance and press the seam open. Repeat on the other side of the middle panel. You will have a finished piece of fabric that measures 68 in/173 cm wide (one 41-in-/104-cm-wide middle panel and two 13½-in-/34-cm-wide side panels).

C   Press out any wrinkles.

STEP 2: HEADBOARD COVERING

A   Work in a well-ventilated room or outside. Lay the drop cloth or newspapers where you will be working.

B   Lay the headboard base on the drop cloth or newspapers, then spray with the spray adhesive. Carefully place the foam piece on the headboard base, and align all edges. Let the adhesive dry.

C   Lay the quilt batting in a single layer, then place the headboard, foam side down, in the center of the batting. Depending on the size and weight of the headboard, this may be a two-person job. Wrap the excess batting around the edges of the headboard and staple to the headboard base about 1 in/2.5 cm from the edge, pulling the batting taut and smooth. When you get to any corners or curves, fold or pleat the batting on the back of the headboard so the look from the front is smooth and wrinkle free.

D   Lay the pieced fabric in a single layer, **wrong**-side up. Place the headboard, batting side down, in the center. Make sure the headboard is perfectly centered on the pieced fabric, using the ruler or tape measure if necessary. Wrap the excess fabric around the edges of the headboard, and staple it to the headboard base about 1½ in/4 cm from the edge, pulling the fabric taut and smooth. When you get to any corners or curves, fold or pleat the fabric on the back so the look from the front is smooth and wrinkle free. Trim away any excess batting or fabric. The back of the headboard won't look great, but you won't see it once it is mounted to your wall.

STEP 3: FINISHING

A   Using the power drill with screw bits and smaller screws, secure the flush mounts or French cleat to the back of your headboard.

B   Determine the placement of the mount/s on your wall, and secure the mount/s with the longer screws. Hang the headboard.

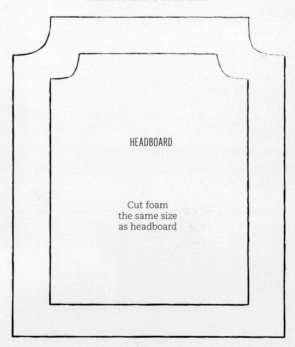

* SKETCH FOR CUTTING *

Cut batting and fabric
at least 4 in/10 cm larger
than headboard on all sides

HEADBOARD

Cut foam
the same size
as headboard

№ 21

Dream a Little Dream Canopy Panache

Lying under this sweet canopy will make you drift off to slumber peacefully every night. What girl could resist an ultrafeminine addition like this? This is a fairly simple project, so consider making different canopies to change with the seasons—pick a rich color for fall and winter, then lighten things up for spring and summer.

NOTE: See illustration on page 171 for placement of hardware in photo. Placement can vary depending on height of ceiling and size of bed.

Finished size:

Fabric gathered to 16 in/40.5 cm wide at the top. Fabric is 42 in/ 107 cm wide at hem. The canopy length will pool at the floor quite a bit.

MATERIALS

- 8 yd/7.3 m printed mid-weight cotton fabric (45 in/114 cm wide) for Canopy
- 7 yd/6.5 m coordinating solid mid-weight cotton fabric (45 in/114 cm wide) for Lining
- One 16-in/40.5-cm wooden dowel (1 in/2.5 cm diameter)
- One 6-in/15-cm L bracket or corner brace
- 2 medallion curtain holdbacks
- Screws to attach L bracket to dowel
- Screws to attach curtain holdbacks to wall
- Heavyweight screws appropriate for your type of wall, to attach L-bracket

FROM THE SEWING BASKET

- Water-soluble fabric marker
- Ruler
- Pins
- Scissors for fabric
- Small-gauge string or crochet cotton

FROM THE CRAFT CABINET

- Pencil
- Tape measure
- Power drill and drill bits
- Screwdriver

CUTTING

FROM CANOPY FABRIC:

Cut off ¾ yd/70 cm from the end of the fabric. Fold this piece in half, with **right** sides together, and align along the selvage edges. Using the fabric marker and the ruler, draw the dimensions below onto the wrong side of the fabric.

Cut eight 3-by-42-in/7.5-by-107-cm rectangles, on the fold, for Ruffle.

Cut both selvage edges off the remaining Canopy fabric.

FROM LINING FABRIC:

Cut both selvage edges off the Lining fabric.

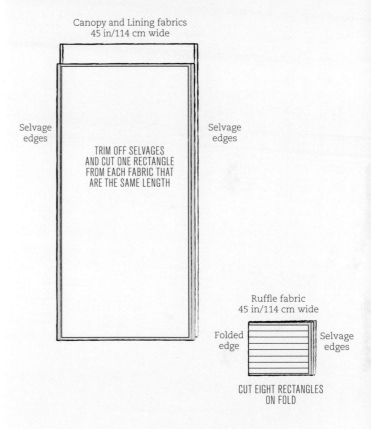

* FABRIC LAYOUT DIAGRAM *

Canopy and Lining fabrics
45 in/114 cm wide

Selvage edges

Selvage edges

TRIM OFF SELVAGES
AND CUT ONE RECTANGLE
FROM EACH FABRIC THAT
ARE THE SAME LENGTH

Ruffle fabric
45 in/114 cm wide

Folded edge

Selvage edges

CUT EIGHT RECTANGLES
ON FOLD

FOR BOTH FABRICS:

With the Canopy and Lining fabrics **right**-sides together and aligned along the long edges, trim off any excess Canopy fabric so they are the same length. Also make sure that both of the short ends are trimmed so they are squared with the long edges.

ASSEMBLE

STEP 1: HARDWARE

A   Place the top of the L bracket along the dowel. You want 1 end of the dowel to be flush against the wall. Screw the L bracket to the dowel.

B   Decide on placement of the L bracket and screw it to the wall, making sure to use the appropriate type of screw for your wall.

C   Decide on the placement of the holdbacks and screw them to your wall.

STEP 2: RUFFLE AND CANOPY.

A   Place 2 of the Ruffle pieces **right** sides together, align along 1 short end, and pin. Sew together with a ¼-in/6-mm seam allowance. Continue in the same manner until all the Ruffle pieces are joined into 1 long strip. Press all the seams open. Then fold the entire Ruffle in half lengthwise with **wrong** sides together, align the raw edges, and press.

B   Follow the instructions for gathering method two *(page 23)* along the raw edges of the Ruffle. Don't pull the string to gather. Fold the Ruffle piece in half, align the short ends, and place a pin at the fold to mark the center of the Ruffle length.

C   Fold the Canopy piece in half, align the short ends, and place a pin at the fold to mark the center. With the Canopy piece **right**-side up on a flat surface, match the center pin of the Ruffle with the center pin of the Canopy, and pin the pieces together, aligning the raw edges. Pin the Ruffle ends to each end of the Canopy piece, then start pulling the string to gather the Ruffle so it is the same length as the Canopy. These gathers will be pretty loose and not that close together. Distribute the Ruffle gathers evenly, pinning as needed. Once you are happy with the Ruffle gathers, baste the Ruffle to the Canopy, ³⁄₈ in/1 cm from the raw edges. Clip the gathering string in a few places and pull out to remove. Lightly press the Ruffle so that the folded edge is lying nicely along the long edge of the Canopy.

D   With **right** sides together, align all raw edges of the Canopy and Lining pieces and pin. The Ruffle should be sandwiched between these 2 layers. Sew together with ½-in/12-mm seam allowance, pivoting at the corners and leaving a 20-in/50-cm opening along 1 short end. Trim the corners and turn the entire piece **right**-side out through opening. Press all edges flat, and then press the edges of the opening under ½ in/12 mm.

E   Edge stitch *(page 21)* around the perimeter of the Canopy, making sure to close the opening as you go.

STEP 3: CASING

A   Fold the entire Canopy piece in half, with the Lining sides together, and align all edges. With the fabric marker and the ruler, draw a straight line across the width of the fabric, 3 in/7.5 cm from the fold. Then draw a second straight line 2½ in/6 cm below the first. Pin the Canopy together between the 2 lines. Sew along each of these lines. *(See illustration.)*

B   Place the casing over the dowel, gathering it up as you go. Drape the ends of the Canopy over the curtain holdbacks and admire your handiwork!

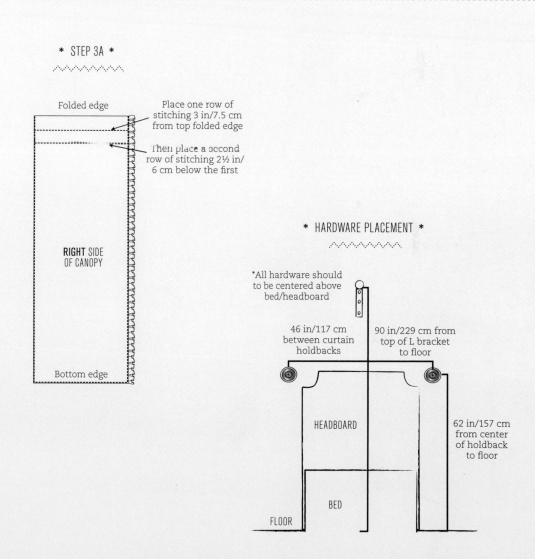

* STEP 3A *

Folded edge

Place one row of stitching 3 in/7.5 cm from top folded edge

Then place a second row of stitching 2½ in/ 6 cm below the first

RIGHT SIDE OF CANOPY

Bottom edge

* HARDWARE PLACEMENT *

*All hardware should to be centered above bed/headboard

46 in/117 cm between curtain holdbacks

90 in/229 cm from top of L bracket to floor

62 in/157 cm from center of holdback to floor

HEADBOARD

BED

FLOOR

Resources

SEWING, CRAFT, AND DECORATING SUPPLIES

3D WOOD CRAFT
www.3dwoodcraft.com/index.html
Wooden letters and signs.

AFLORAL
www.afloral.com
Silk flowers.

ALDIK
www.aldikhome.com
Silk flowers.

ALLCRAFT SUPPLIES
www.allcraftsupplies.com
Handles for tote bags and other assorted craft supplies.

ART GLITTER
www.artglitter.com
Glitter used on letters for banner.

AURORA SLEEP PRODUCTS
http://aurorapillow.com
Pillow forms and inserts.

BRASWELL GALLERIES
www.braswellgalleries.com
Furniture and lacquer services.

COATS AND CLARK
www.coatsandclark.com
Wide range of colorful yarns and threads, as well as other sewing supplies.

CREATE FOR LESS
www.createforless.com
Wide variety of sewing notions and supplies; chipboard scalloped circles and other shapes; clear template plastic for quilt templates and other quilting notions.

DARK HORSE FARM DESIGNS
http://darkhorsefarmdesigns.com
Custom quilts and baby quilts.

DICK BLICK ART MATERIALS
www.dickblick.com
Tracing paper by the roll and other assorted craft supplies.

DRAPERY SEWING SUPPLIES
www.draperysewingsupplies.com
Supplies for drapery, including Deep Pleat Tape and four-prong long-necked pleat hooks.

FOAM BY MAIL
www.foambymail.com/index.html
Foam pet beds and other foam supplies.

FOAM 'N MORE AND UPHOLSTERY
www.foamforyou.com
Foam sheets.

FRAMA SEWING
http://framasewing.blogspot.com
Custom window treatments, slipcovers, upholstery, pillows, cushions, and bedding.

LUNA BAZAAR
www.lunabazaar.com
Paper lanterns in a variety of sizes and colors.

MAYA ROAD
http://mayaroad.net
Chipboard alphabet and other decorative sets.

MILLIE RAE'S
www.millieraesstore.blogspot.com
Vintage home decor.

ROWLEY COMPANY
www.rowleycompany.com/welcome.asp
FirmaFlex, curtain hardware, down bedding, pillows, and upholstery supplies.

RUFFLED BENCH
http://bebepapillon.com
Papillon linens for bed skirts, curtains, upholstery, and more.

SAVE ON CRAFTS
www.save-on-crafts.com
Craft supplies, balloons, paper lanterns, and more.

STOVER QUALITY QUILTING
www.stoverquilting.com
Mail-order machine quilting service.

TINSEL TRADING COMPANY
www.tinseltrading.com/index.php
Wide range of high-quality notions and sewing supplies, including metal fabrics, fringes, and vintage flowers.

A TREASURE NEST
www.atreasurenest.com/default.aspx
Appliqués, fashion and home decor accessories, trims, and notions.

VICKI PAYNE DESIGN
http://freespiritfabric.com
Cotton, cotton poplin, and cotton flannel fabrics.

WEDDING STAR
Weddingstar.com
Just Fluff pom-poms.

WESTMINSTER FIBERS
www.westminsterfabrics.com OR
http://freespiritfabric.com
Huge assortment of designer fabrics.

ZIPPERSTOP
www.zipperstop.com
Wide variety of zippers, Hug Snug seam binding, and other notions.

SIS BOOM PRODUCTS AND FABRICS

PEKING HANDICRAFT
1388 San Mateo Avenue
South San Francisco, CA 94080
650-871-3788
http://pkhc.com/
Assortment of Sis Boom aprons, rugs, and pillows (wholesale).

SCIENTIFIC SEAMSTRESS
http://scientificseamstress.com
High-quality patterns and detailed sewing "protocols" in electronic format.

SWAK EMBROIDERY.COM
http://swakembroidery.com
Good selection of machine embroidery designs, including Sis Boom motifs.

WESTMINSTER FIBERS
www.westminsterfabrics.com OR
http://freespiritfabric.com
Huge assortment of designer fabrics.

YOU CAN MAKE THIS
www.youcanmakethis.com/index.htm
Great source for patterns and instructions, including Sis Boom patterns available for instant download.

Contributors

BEATA BASIK
Crocheted Pillowcase
rosehip.typepad.com

JANIS BULLIS CREATIVE SERVICES
Fabric Covered Boxes
Creative Services
20 Shuit Place
Central Valley, NY 10917
845-928-2170
jbullis@frontiernet.net

NANCY GEANEY QUILT
Madeline Quilt
www.darkhorsefarmdesigns.
blogspot.com

TAMMY GILLEY STUDIOS
Millie's Market Tote
tammygilley.com

ARTWORK

BARBARA SRAWSER ART
*Jen O'Conner represents
Barbara Strawser's work at*
www.earthangelstoys.com.
www.strawserart.com/barbara

CHARITY

CUFCAKES
*Fun clothing embellishments in
support of charity*
www.cufcakes.com

**FOOD/EDIBLE TABLE DECOR
TOPPINGS**
Cupcakes
www.toppingscupcakes.com

TIME FOR LYME
www.timeforlyme.org

Credits

DOLIN O'SHEA
Patterns, instructions, and illustrations
www.lulubliss.com

MADELINE RHODES
*Wardrobe stylist
Model manager*
www.leanandchic.com

MARY TUCCIARONE
Home interior stylist
tuccidesignllc@aol.com

NANCY GEANEY
Photo stylist
www.darkhorsefarmdesigns.
blogspot.com

RONNIE STAM
Hairstylist
www.kramerkramer.com

TIM GEANEY
Photographer
www.timgeaney.com

CONSULTANTS

JORDAN RABIDOU
Internet marketing strategy
www.theheavenlyhash.com

MADELINE RHODES & DEBRA WOLF
www.leanandchic.com

MARCELLA KOVAC
Girl's World, Website Continuity
www.thebananaland.com

**PERSONAL THANK-YOU'S
WITH LOVE FROM JENNIFER:**
My mom forever and ever; my sissies
and bro; Tim and Nancy Geaney; Mary
Tucciarone; Maritza Bermudez; Betty Ann
Patsenka; Madeline Rhodes; and Bill W.

**FOR THEIR COMMITMENT TO DESIGN
AND LOVE OF THE CAPTURED MOMENT:**
Dolin O'Shea, for her technical expertise
and overall sweetness; Donna Wilder,
my mentor; our models, baby Carly,
and our neighbors—we adore you; my
agent, Jill Cohen; the folks at Chronicle
Books, including Jodi Warshaw, Laura Lee
Mattingly, Lisa Tauber, Kate Woodrow,
Lorraine Woodcheke, Michelle Clair, Claire
Fletcher, Molly Jones, and Aya Akazawa;
Westminster Fabrics; Joyce Robertson;
Nancy Jewell; Elyse Mullis; Leann Spadaro;
Alberto Santos; our network of fabric
suppliers and sellers; Carla Crim for our
PDF patterns; Roberto Sancho, puppeteer;
Amanda Sakamoto, fabulous intern; our
Twitter and Facebook community; and
our diehard fans. Big hugs to you all!

Index

Sis Boom
JENNIFER PAGANELLI

For Sis Boom updates and happenings, The Sis Boom Lookbook,
Sis Boom Shop, and more, visit www.sisboom.com

Clothing Patterns in this book are available at sisboom.com
or retailers specified on our blog

Many of the silhouettes seen in this book are available in the
Sis Boom Patterns section www.sisboom.com/patterns

Flickr is a great way to see Sis Boom projects made by Sis Boom fans!
http://www.flickr.com/groups/458917@N25/

Keep in touch with Jennifer on Twitter!
www.twitter.com/sisboom

Find out more about Sis Boom on Facebook!
Daily updates to keep our fans in the loop!
www.facebook.com/sisboom